INSIDE THE ASYLUM

INSIDE THE ASYLUM

Why the UN and Old Europe Are Worse Than You Think

JED BABBIN

Since 1947
REGNERY
PUBLISHING, INC.
An Eagle Publishing Company • Washington, DC

Library of Congress Cataloging-in-Publication Data on file with the Library of Congress

ISBN 0-89526-088-3

Published in the United States by
Regnery Publishing, Inc.
An Eagle Publishing Company
One Massachusetts Avenue, NW
Washington, DC 20001

Visit us at www.regnery.com

Distributed to the trade by
National Book Network
4720-A Boston Way
Lanham, MD 20706

Printed on acid-free paper
Manufactured in the United States of America
10 9 8 7 6 5 4 3 2 1

Books are available in quantity for promotional or premium use. Write to Director of Special Sales, Regnery Publishing, Inc., One Massachusetts Avenue, NW, Washington, DC 20001, for information on discounts and terms, or call (202) 216-0600.

I dedicate this book to an unknown American. I saw this man only for a moment on September 11, 2001. The television crews massing near the fallen World Trade Center were interviewing everyone who came within range of their microphones. Clad in blue jeans and a T-shirt, topped by a construction worker's hard hat, the man was walking purposefully toward the disaster. When the reporter asked him, "What are you going to do when you get there?" he looked ahead and replied, "Whatever they need me to do." That man and millions of other Americans just like him are the strength of this great nation.

CONTENTS

CHAPTER ONE
Welcome to the Asylum
1

CHAPTER TWO
The UN: Handmaiden of Terrorism
7

CHAPTER THREE
"Kofigate": The UN Oil-for-Food Program
23

CHAPTER FOUR
Quagmire Diplomacy
33

CHAPTER FIVE
Secretary-General Kofi Annan: A Symptom of the UN Disease
39

CHAPTER SIX
The UN Bureaucracy: Nice Work If You Can Get It
49

CHAPTER SEVEN
The UN's Fatal Flaws
57

CHAPTER EIGHT
Clinton's Classroom
71

CHAPTER NINE
UN Reform: A Fool's Errand
79

CHAPTER TEN
The Death of Old Europe
93

CHAPTER ELEVEN
The EUnuchs and Their Union
109

CHAPTER TWELVE
NATO and the EUnuch Military
119

CHAPTER THIRTEEN
Forward Together, or Not
139

ACKNOWLEDGMENTS
145

APPENDIX
147

NOTES
177

INDEX
185

CHAPTER ONE

WELCOME TO THE ASYLUM

*"The UN is now a central problem for the world,
because we take too much notice of it."*

—British historian Paul Johnson

IF THE DEMOCRATIC PARTY OF JOHN KERRY AND HILLARY CLINTON HAS its way, UN secretary-general Kofi Annan and French president Jacques Chirac will hold a veto over American foreign policy. The Kerry-Clinton Democrats believe that America's national security and foreign policy should be made subservient to the United Nations and Old Europe in the name of "multilateralism." Gone will be George W. Bush's decisive "unilateral" defense of American interests. Instead, we will have multilateral inaction, terrorism treated as a matter for the police and the courts, and our own foreign policy dictated by the UN and the elites of Old Europe. We've been down this road before, during the presidency of Bill Clinton—and we learned that it leads to failure. It leads us farther from security for our nation, and farther from victory against terrorists and the nations that support them.

One definition of insanity is doing the same thing, in the same way, over and over again and expecting different results. In the asylum that the United Nations has become, this form of insanity is not suffered by all the inmates. The most severe cases are the democratic countries that always want to give the UN another chance to be what it was supposed to be: a forum for nations of good will to meet and settle disputes peacefully without resort to war. Instead, today's UN is a diplomatic version of the Mad Hatter's tea party, where good is evil, right is wrong, and every dictator and despot is given the same rights and privileges as the leaders of free nations. For the United States, the UN is a quagmire of diplomacy in which wars can be lost but not won, alliances can dissolve but not be formed, the birth of nuclear terrorism is being watched but not aborted, and no adult supervision is imposed on a Third World playground where anti-Americanism is the favorite game.

The UN General Assembly is a gaggle of has-beens and never-wases that believes raiding the U.S. Treasury is its right. The Security Council—supposed to be the strongest force for peace—is interested only in tying down the world's remaining superpower, the United States, and making any American action taken without UN permission illegitimate in the eyes of the world.

President Bush's policy of preempting terrorists—attacking them before they can attack America—depends on more than the superiority of American arms. It depends on surprise, hitting terrorists where they lurk before they have a chance to run. That means the UN is the enemy of preemption. Every time we engage in endless, pointless UN debates, we give up the crucial advantage of surprise. The terrorists know that, and so do our so-called "allies" in Europe.

America and its real allies have toppled two terrorist regimes in spite of the UN, not because of it. If American foreign policy were subordinated to the judgment of the Security Council, the Taliban would be negotiating from its stronghold in Kabul, Saddam would still be in power in Iraq, and the threat of al-Qaeda would be tolerated as the cost of doing business in the twenty-first century. The UN can't aid the fight against terror because its members—in thrall to the rogue nations among them—can't even agree what terrorism is. The UN has become a tool for outlaw nations, their European trading partners, and the tin-pot dictators of the world to constrain American action everywhere, especially in the global war against terrorism. By delaying justice and denying its approval to the forces of good in the fight against evil, the UN functions as a shield for the enemies of freedom.

As I'll show later on, the UN isn't content with its Lilliputian attempts to tie down the American Gulliver. It is also an errand boy for the despots of the world. The UN not only turns a blind eye to terror-ism, but is actually quite comfortable with it, admitting terrorists to the community of nations, tolerating their development of nuclear weapons, and—in at least one of its largest agencies—putting members of terrorist organizations on its payroll.

Hezbollah—the terrorist organization that has more American blood on its hands than any other except al-Qaeda—is entrenched adjacent to UN "peacekeeper" bases on the Israeli-Lebanese border. On page 155, there is a picture taken from an Israeli Defense Force position called Post Tziporen. The picture shows something Israelis see every day, but the media and the world ignore: two flagpoles about fifteen feet apart; on one, the blue UN flag, and on the other, the yellow flag of Hezbollah, bearing an AK-47 assault rifle held in a clenched fist.

An Israeli soldier who served at that IDF post in 2003 described to me what he saw there, how the UN and Hezbollah men go about their daily routines side by side. The Hezbollah—identified by the uniforms and ski masks they wear—use the same telephones, drink the same water, and get along quite nicely with the UN "peace monitors." At Post Tziporen, UN tolerance of terrorism is visible to the naked eye. But this is only one small part of the problem. The UN's tolerance of—and even support for—terrorism is embedded in the minds of all, from the lowliest "peacekeepers" to the highest appointed officials. This acceptance is insidious and pervasive.

Tolerance of terrorism is only one of the UN's unstated noxious norms. Another is financial corruption. The UN's Oil-for-Food program was supposed to allow Saddam Hussein's Iraq to sell oil only for food and medicine to supply the needs of the Iraqi people. But the corruption of the UN allowed Saddam to skim billions of dollars to buy arms, to buy UN Security Council votes, and to bribe politicians and UN officials at the highest levels. Under the UN's supervision, even the small portion of money truly spent on medicine and food was wasted. Much of the food wasn't even, in the words of one program investigator, "fit for pigs."

The UN is not only financially corrupt, but is also morally and intellectually so. During the Iraq campaign, beginning in March 2003, there was, all too often, graphic proof of Iraqi abuse, torture, and murder of American prisoners of war. Did UN secretary-general Kofi Annan condemn Iraq for these atrocities? No. About a week into the war, he admonished *both sides* to treat prisoners of war humanely. Annan's perverse moral relativism is but a symptom of the disease infecting both the UN and Old Europe.

Our national security will be greatly reduced—and our foreign policy chained to false friends and true enemies—if the UN and Old Europe again annex American foreign policy through the tool of the Democratic Party. As former UN ambassador Jeane Kirkpatrick told me, "The issue is whether the UN should have any role in U.S. decisions on the use of force." She added, "There is no ground in the UN Charter or in precedent to support the position that the Security Council is the only source of legitimacy for the use of force.... The importance of American sovereignty over American action is of the utmost importance." According to Ambassador Kirkpatrick, "We must never agree that the U.S. needs the permission of the Security Council or any non-American entity to take action to protect our security. That is an irreducible responsibility and obligation of our government, which of course is responsible to the Congress and the American people as specified in our Constitution."

For the UN to be an arbiter of legitimacy, it would have to first be able to distinguish between right and wrong, between good and evil. But its charter and its membership preclude that. How can any group granting the worst despotisms in the world and the freest and greatest democracies the same standing and rights be a judge of right and wrong? The UN, by its charter, equates Syria with the United States, China with Britain, and the Sudan (where chattel slavery is still practiced) with Israel. What Kofi Annan and the UN demand is that the legitimacy of the decisions and actions of free nations be dependent upon the approval of the despotisms. It is a fraud on the world, and will continue as long as we tolerate it.

What the United States needs to do is reform its alliances to fit reality, rather than the past, and end its membership in the UN. The nations of the West are no longer united by the threat of Soviet expansionism, and the emasculated nations of Old Europe—the EUnuchs—have sunk to a level of decadence unseen since the 1930s. Europe's core values concerning morality, freedom, and defending the West have diverged from where we as Americans stand. Old Europe has returned to a policy of appeasement, refusing to see the threats being born around it, and choosing to abandon the military capacity to deal with them. Old Europe sees America only as an obstacle to its own economic growth, and as a danger to its elegant diplomacy of inaction. While Americans shed blood to fight terrorism, the shopkeepers of Old Europe make special trade deals with terrorist nations.

France, the self-appointed leader of Old Europe, challenges American action on every economic, diplomatic, and military front in order to support its false claim to global power. France is not a global power. It only plays one on television and in the UN. Those who follow France's leadership—Germany, Belgium, and the others who flock to the banner of the European Union—are allying themselves to thwart American decisions in the UN, in NATO, and in the diplomatic fight against such terrorist-sponsoring states as Iran, Syria, and Saudi Arabia.

Given Old Europe's cowardice and greed, NATO's usefulness might be over. And so is the usefulness of the UN.

After the fall of Saddam Hussein—accomplished only because America finally lost patience with the UN—America's crisis of confidence in the UN has grown acute. The Security Council, having passed seventeen resolutions seeking Saddam's disarmament, was utterly incapable of doing what the UN Charter says it should: enforce its resolutions to keep the peace. If the UN cannot be relied upon to fulfill its own purpose, why should American taxpayers spend more than $7 billion *every year* to sustain it?

Even UN secretary-general Kofi Annan knows that something has to give. In September 2003, he told the Security Council, "Excellencies, we have come to a fork in the road. This may be a moment no less decisive than 1945 itself, when the UN was founded." This book will demonstrate that America, too, is at a crossroads. And the path we need to take leads us out of the UN.

CHAPTER TWO

THE UN: HANDMAIDEN OF TERRORISM

"The Security Council decides that all States shall . . . refrain from providing any sort of support . . . to entities . . . involved in terrorist acts . . . , take the necessary steps to prevent the commission of terrorist acts . . . , [and] deny safe haven to those who finance, plan, support or commit terrorist acts."

—UN Security Council Resolution 1373, passed in response to the September 11, 2001, attacks on the United States

BY SIGNING THE UN CHARTER, EVERY MEMBER NATION AGREES TO accept and carry out the resolutions of the Security Council.[1] But the democracies of the world are the only members that ever do. In fact, even UN agencies trusted to carry out the resolutions usually either ignore them or work to violate them. The best example is the UN's nuclear watchdog, the International Atomic Energy Agency (IAEA).

The UN as Midwife to the Birth of Nuclear Terrorism

Mohamed ElBaradei is the UN's head of the IAEA. The agency is supposed to inspect atomic energy programs to make sure they don't violate bans on nuclear weapons proliferation. But like his boss, Secretary-General Kofi Annan, ElBaradei is willfully blind to the facts.

Ever since the radical Islamic takeover in 1979, Iran has been fever-
ishly working to produce nuclear weapons, all the while denying and
concealing its intent and its work. At a November 2003 *American Spectator* dinner, Undersecretary of State John Bolton took the IAEA to task:

> To date, three reports by... the International Atomic Energy
> Agency have established that Iran is in violation—in multi-
> ple instances—of its safeguards obligations under the
> Nuclear Non-Proliferation Treaty. While Iran has consis-
> tently denied any program to develop nuclear weapons, the
> IAEA has amassed an enormous amount of evidence to the
> contrary that makes this assertion increasingly implausible.
>
> After extensive documentation of Iran's denials and
> deceptions over an eighteen-year period, and a long litany
> of serious violations of Iran's commitments to the IAEA,
> the [latest IAEA] report nonetheless concluded that "no
> evidence" had been found of an Iranian nuclear weapons
> program. I must say that the report's assertion is simply
> impossible to believe. This is not only the administration's
> view. Thomas Cochran, a scientist with the Natural
> Resources Defense Council, told the *New York Times* that
> "it's dumbfounding that the IAEA, after saying that Iran
> for eighteen years had a secret effort to enrich uranium
> and separate plutonium, would turn around and say there
> was no evidence of a nuclear weapons program. If that's
> not evidence, I don't know what is." Gary Samore, a for-
> mer Clinton administration official now with the Interna-
> tional Institute of Strategic Studies in London, told the
> *London Telegraph* that "this is unquestionably a bomb
> program."

The United States believes that the massive and covert
Iranian effort to acquire sensitive nuclear capabilities makes

sense only as part of a nuclear weapons program. Iran is trying to legitimize as "peaceful and transparent" its pursuit of nuclear fuel cycle capabilities that would give it the ability to produce fissile material for nuclear weapons. This includes uranium mining and extraction, uranium conversion and enrichment, reactor fuel fabrication, heavy water production, a heavy water reactor well suited for plutonium production, and "management" of spent fuel—a euphemism for reprocessing spent fuel to recover plutonium. The recent IAEA report confirms that Iran has been engaged in all of these activities over many years, and that it deliberately and repeatedly lied to the IAEA about it.

The international community now has to determine whether Iran has come clean on this program and how to react to the large number of serious violations to which Iran has admitted. . . . If it is continuing to conceal its nuclear program and has again lied to the IAEA, the international community must be prepared to declare Iran in noncompliance with its IAEA safeguards obligations.[2]

Bolton's proofs are conclusive: The IAEA is blind because it refuses to see. Because the IAEA refuses to see, the reality of a nuclear-armed Iran grows closer every day, and with it grows the danger of nuclear terrorism.

Last year, a delegation from the European Union—hoping to avert a diplomatic crisis between the United States and Iran, and anxious to befriend Iran for its oil—negotiated an expanded inspection plan for Iran's nuclear program. Under this agreement, Iran promised to allow IAEA inspectors unfettered access to its nuclear facilities, along the lines of the "anywhere, any time" no-notice inspections that Saddam Hussein's regime agreed to in the 1991 cease-fire closing the first Gulf War. But, just as Saddam before them, the Iranians immediately reneged on the deal. And both the IAEA and the EUnuchs remain content with this sort of "progress."

While the IAEA closes its eyes to Iran's nuclear weapons program, its director general is more interested in the "security deficit" he sees between the nuclear haves and the have-nots. In a February 12, 2004, op-ed in the *New York Times*, ElBaradei wrote:

> [A] fundamental part of the non-proliferation bargain is the commitment of the five nuclear states recognized under the non-proliferation treaty—Britain, China, France, Russia and the United States—to move toward disarmament. Recent agreements between Russia and the United States are commendable, but they should be verifiable and irreversible. A clear road map for nuclear disarmament should be established—starting with a major reduction in the 30,000 nuclear warheads still in existence, and bringing into force the long-awaited Comprehensive Nuclear Test Ban Treaty....
>
> We must also begin to address the root causes of insecurity. In areas of longstanding conflict like the Middle East, South Asia, and the Korean Peninsula, the pursuit of weapons of mass destruction—while never justified—can be expected as long as we fail to introduce alternatives that redress the security deficit. We must abandon the unworkable notion that it is morally reprehensible for some countries to pursue weapons of mass destruction yet morally acceptable for others to rely on them for security—and indeed to continue to refine their capacities and postulate plans for their use.

To ElBaradei, there is no difference between American or British possession of nuclear weapons and North Korea's possession of them. The greatest threat of the use of nuclear weapons comes—directly and indirectly—from terror-sponsoring states such as Iran. Iran's leaders have announced that obtaining nuclear weapons is—to them—a religious obligation. Defense sources told me that Iran might already have three nuclear weapons purchased from former Soviet satellite states. Iranian missiles—a substantial number of them highly capable Scud derivatives that could be mated to nuclear weapons—can reach most of the Middle East and soon will have the ability to reach all of Europe, even as far as the United Kingdom.

Iran supports many of the most dangerous terrorist organizations, including Hezbollah and other regional terrorist bands, but most important is its alliance with al-Qaeda and global terrorism. Iran admits that several al-Qaeda leaders are in Iran, but it won't surrender them to face justice because its goals and values are those of the terrorists. Once it can, Iran will arm terrorists with nuclear weapons, and then it is only a matter of time until one is smuggled into the United States and detonated, causing hundreds of thousands of casualties. If we suffer a nuclear September 11, al-Qaeda and its Iranian allies will almost certainly have carried out the attack.

The Iranian mullahs have already said that if they had nuclear weapons, they would use them on Israel. In 1981, Israeli aircraft knocked out Saddam Hussein's nuclear program in the Osirak raid. But Iran's nuclear programs are, according to intelligence sources, dispersed among several sites—some of them hardened and underground—that aren't susceptible to such an attack.

If the IAEA—and the EU—joined the U.S. to create an international consensus to compel Iran to surrender its nuclear program, there is a remote possibility that the mullahs would comply. But in the absence of that consensus, the only defense against Iran's nuclear arms program is American action, which needs to include unrelenting diplomatic and economic pressure, and serious covert operations to topple the mullahs' regime. We cannot afford to wait for the IAEA to act, because the IAEA merely reflects the corruption of the UN.

The UN as a Base of Operation for Terrorists in the United States

UN delegations themselves are a constant source of concern. In June 2002, two Iranian "diplomats" were caught casing the Statue of Liberty and were expelled.[3] The statue is one of the announced targets of al-Qaeda. In November 2003, two more Iranians working for the Iranian UN mission were caught videotaping a New York subway in Queens, New York, and also were expelled.[4] Many foreign diplomats use their American UN base to conduct espionage activities in the United States.

Case in point: On November 19, 2002, the Benevolence International Foundation (BIF) was designated a terrorist organization by the U.S. Treasury Department.[5] Apparently founded by Mohammed Jamal Khalifa, a brother-in-law of Osama bin Laden, the BIF moved its headquarters to the United States in March 1992.[6] In the 1990s, it operated in Bosnia under the name of Bosanska Idealna Futura, funneling money and munitions to al-Qaeda and other terrorists. Enaam Arnaout, its director, was later indicted in the United States for terrorist activities.

According to Global Information Systems, an intelligence and news analysis organization, when Huso Zivalj became Bosnia-Herzegovina's ambassador to the United Nations in January 2001, he secretly and illegally gave special UN status to Saffet Catovic in New York, giving him a yellow UN pass. (Red passes are for attachés and other diplomats, up to first secretary; yellow is reserved for the ambassador, permanent representative, or deputy permanent representative.) This allowed Catovic free access to the UN buildings. Zivalj kept this information secret, largely because it was illegal.[7]

According to Steve Emerson of The Investigative Project, Catovic quickly became one of the BIF's spokesmen and fund-raisers,[8] and even lectured at a "jihad camp" in Pennsylvania.[9]

Evan Kohlmann, senior terrorism consultant for The Investigative Project, summed it up this way:

> Throughout the 1990s, various international terrorist organizations were able to manipulate UN agencies and resources

around the world in order to support their... goals. Some of these international diplomatic bodies, including even the United Nations headquarters in New York, have been infiltrated by known supporters of terrorism—who... provided tactical information to a terror cell targeting that very same complex in 1994. Similarly, foreign intelligence officers masquerading as UN diplomats have been able to use their status of immunity to conduct reconnaissance on other potential terrorist targets in the northeast.

Espionage activities in the UN are nothing new, and the UN's tolerance of espionage and terrorism is old and systemic, and includes granting "observer" status to Yassir Arafat's Palestinian Authority, which is encouraged, in the words of the UN, "to participate as observers in the sessions and the work of the General Assembly" and to maintain "permanent offices at [UN] Headquarters." Terrorists, to the UN, are acceptable UN observers because terrorism, to the UN, is not easily defined; it is in the eye of the beholder.

The UN's Free Pass to Terrorists

The UN's Counter-Terrorism Committee is composed of the entire Security Council. It was created by Resolution 1373 on September 28, 2001.[10] The resolution requires all UN member states to deny support to terrorists, to cooperate in finding and arresting them, and generally sets out the terms with which terrorism should be dealt. But it doesn't define what terrorism is, because the UN can't agree. And that makes the resolution—and its requirements—virtually meaningless.

As Israel's ambassador to the United States, Daniel Ayalon, told me, "Right now, in the International Court of Justice," there is an attempt "to bring Israel to trial because of certain self-defense measures we have to take, because of the [Palestinian terrorist] attacks. But they [the International Court of Justice] will not try terrorism, specifically suicide bombing, which I think is the plague of our time. And why not?

Because it's outside their jurisdiction. You cannot try anybody in international courts for terrorism. You know why? Because they can't even define terrorism."

Ayalon continued, "You come to this body—the UN—which is supposed to be the lightning rod for morality, [and yet] you cannot pass a resolution or find a definition for terrorism." He added, "When there was an attempt to have a very short, objective definition—with no political connotations attached—you will not have that because the Arab countries will not have that pass."

The UN debate on defining terrorism hasn't established anything other than a convenient excuse for inaction. Some states—and non-states, such as the Palestinian Authority—insist that the definition exclude attacks on military targets, which is absurd. Under that definition, the September 11, 2001, attack on the Pentagon wasn't terrorism.

Actually, defining terrorism is easy. All the UN had to do was adopt the definition of terrorism that is already implicit in international law: The Geneva Convention defines a "lawful combatant" and—by exclusion—defines terrorism.

Under the Geneva Convention for the Treatment of Prisoners of War, the major nations that comprise the UN Security Council have agreed on those who are "lawful combatants"—that is, those who are entitled to protection as prisoners of war. The definition of lawful combatants includes, among others, those who are:

- Members of the armed forces of a party to the conflict, including militias or volunteer corps forming part of such armed forces
- Members of other militias and members of other volunteer corps, including those of organized resistance movements, belonging to a party to the conflict and operating in or outside their own territory, provided that they fulfill the following conditions: First, being commanded by a person responsible for his subordinates, second, having a fixed dis-

tinctive sign recognizable at a distance, third, carrying arms openly, and fourth, conducting their operations in accordance with the laws and customs of war.

- Members of regular armed forces who profess allegiance to a government or an authority not recognized by the detaining power
- Persons who accompany the armed forces without actually being members thereof, such as civilian members of military aircraft crews, war correspondents, supply contractors, members of labor units or of services responsible for the welfare of the armed forces, provided that they have received authorization from the armed forces which they accompany
- Members of crews of the merchant marine and the crews of civil aircraft of the parties to the conflict
- Inhabitants of a non-occupied territory, who on the approach of the enemy spontaneously take up arms to resist the invading forces, without having had time to form themselves into regular armed units, provided they carry arms openly and respect the laws and customs of war[11]

Terrorists fail to meet almost all of these criteria and thus are not protected by the Geneva Convention. They are, therefore, outlaws under the law of war. By refusing to use the definition that already exists, the Security Council is blocking any UN action against terrorism. And by creating that obstacle, the UN makes a peaceful solution to terrorism much less likely.

If the UN agreed on a definition for terrorism—and thereby created a basis for deciding which nations are terrorist nations—it could take peaceful action against terrorist states through economic sanctions such as trade embargos, restrictions on the transfer of funds, and restrictions on the free movement of people from terrorist states. Short of such international action—which the UN won't take because terrorism is practiced and supported by several UN members—war becomes the only option.

Defining terrorism is not an academic exercise. Moqtadr Sadr, a minor Shiite cleric, has ordered his terrorist "militia" to kill Americans in Iraq. When the U.S.-led coalition forced Sadr's "newspaper" to stop publishing, Senator John Kerry said, "They shut a newspaper that belongs to a legitimate voice in Iraq . . . Well, let me . . . change the term 'legitimate.' It belongs to a voice—because he has clearly taken on a far more radical tone in recent days and aligned himself with both Hamas and Hezbollah, which is a sort of terrorist alignment." If direct alliance with Hamas and Hezbollah—in addition to being funded by Iran, which Sadr is—is only "sort of" a terrorist alignment in Kerry's viewpoint, what could Sadr possibly do to qualify himself as a terrorist? We'll never learn that answer from the UN.

Part of the reason, of course, is the sheer moral relativism of the UN. But another part is the UN's long love affair with Yassir Arafat and Palestinian terrorism.

Yassir Arafat: The UN's Favorite Terrorist

On November 13, 1974, Arafat addressed the UN General Assembly for the first time. "The old world order is crumbling before our eyes," he said, "as imperialism, colonialism, neo-colonialism and racism, the chief form of which is Zionism, ineluctably perish." Arafat said he was a "revolutionary;" his opponents were the "terrorists":

> The difference between the revolutionary and the terrorist lies in the reason for which each fights. For whoever stands by a just cause and fights for the freedom and liberation of his land from the invaders, the settlers, and the colonialists, cannot possibly be called terrorist, otherwise the American people in their struggle for liberation from the British colonialists would have been terrorists; the European resistance against the Nazis would be terrorism, the struggle of the Asian, African, and Latin American peoples would also be terrorism, and many of you who are in this Assembly hall

were considered terrorists...As to those who fight against
the just causes, those who wage war to occupy, colonize,
and oppress other people, those are the terrorists. Those are
the people whose actions should be condemned, who should
be called war criminals: for the justice of the cause deter-
mines the right to struggle.[12]

To insist, as the UN has done for thirty years, that Arafat and the
Palestinian Authority are not themselves terrorists is simply to perform
for them the same service that the IAEA is performing for Iran. According to an excerpt I saw from a confidential Israeli report, there have
been more than nineteen thousand attacks on Israelis since Arafat's
intifada began in September 2000: more than twenty-five a day.
According to that report, almost nine hundred Israelis have been killed,
and nearly six thousand wounded in the terrorist attacks.

In October 2003, I interviewed Ziad abu Ziad, a senior advisor to the
Palestinian Authority and formerly its "minister of state." Ziad is an edu-
cated man. Well dressed and well spoken, he is a Westernized face of terrorism. We spoke at length about the 1993 Oslo Accords, under which
the Palestinians promised to end their acts and support of terrorism.

Ziad refers to terrorists as "activists"—a moral equivalency that the
UN, because of its large membership of unsavory Third World dictatorships, and Old Europe, because of its hunger for Arab oil, too often
accept. He and the other Palestinians I met with accept no responsibility for the failure of the Oslo Accords. He bragged—falsely—that from
about 1996 to 2000, the Palestinian Authority ended terrorism. I asked
Ziad why it didn't do so now. "Because we didn't get anything for it,"
he told me. For Ziad and Arafat, the destruction of Israel is the goal
and terrorism is the tool.

A host of terrorist organizations—including Hezbollah, Hamas,
Islamic Jihad and Arafat's own Al-Aqsa Martyrs' Brigade—work with
and through the Palestinian Authority. Photographs and documents
seized by the Israeli army during its 2002 incursion into Arafat's

Ramallah compound showed that Saddam Hussein was funding terrorism against Israel through the Palestinian Authority. Money to support Palestinian terrorist activities was also donated by Iran, Syria, and Saudi Arabia.[13] Most of the financial transactions were performed through the Arab Liberation Front and the Palestinian Liberation Front, headed by Abu al-Abbas, the same man who was briefly the Palestinian "prime minister."[14]

Among the documents the Israelis found were copies of checks paid through the Palestinian Authority to the families of the terrorist bombers. Typical, in the words of the Israeli report, is a check for $25,000, drawn on the Palestinian Investment Bank, payable to "Khaldiya Isma'il Abd al-Aziz al-Hurani, the mother of Hamas terrorist Fuad Isma'il Ahmad al-Hurani, who carried out a suicide attack on 9 March 2002 in the *Moment* café in Jerusalem. 11 Israelis were killed and 16 wounded in the attack."[15]

Separating "mainstream" Palestinian organizations from terrorist groups is impossible. In 2003, the United States imposed a requirement that Palestinian non-governmental organizations (NGOs) certify that none of the money they received would be passed through to terrorists. According to a statement by Azmi al-Shuabi, the chairman of the Palestinian economics affairs committee, Palestinian NGOs received about $30 million in 2003 from USAID alone. They all refused to sign the certification.[16]

The UN doesn't even try to make such distinctions, because it believes that money given by Saddam Hussein, Syria, Iran, and Saudi Arabia to Palestinian suicide bombers was and is money given to a just cause.

The UN's Salaried Terrorists

The UN's High Commissioner for Human Rights is supposed to "lead the international human rights movement by acting as a moral authority and voice for victims."[17] Ireland's Mary Robinson was the commissioner from 1997 to 2002. She set the tone for UN dealings with Palestinian terrorism by telling the world that their cause was just, so their methods were to be excused. Under Robinson, the UN Human Rights Commission sanctioned the use of "all available means" to fight Israel.[18]

The UN Relief and Works Agency for Palestinian Refugees in the Near East (UNRWA) is under the control of the high commissioner. UNRWA bills itself as "the main provider of basic services—education, health, relief, and social services—to over 4.1 million registered Palestine refugees in the Middle East."[19] It also employs terrorists.

In a sworn statement, Professor Rashid Khalidi of the University of Chicago testified that:

> Humanitarian and charitable institutions throughout Palestine employ personnel regardless of sectarian or political affiliation and offer services on a similar basis. Thus, UNRWA, NGO-run and public hospitals and clinics, for example, employ members of different political groups such as Fatah, the PFLP [Popular Front for the Liberation of Palestine], Hamas and Islamic Jihad, without reference to their belonging to a specific group.[20]

But al-Fatah, the PFLP, Hamas, and Islamic Jihad aren't merely political groups, the Palestinian equivalents of the Sierra Club or the Ripon Society. They are terrorist groups.

One of UNRWA's principal duties is to report terrorist activities it encounters. It utterly fails in that duty and—worse still—it appears to abet the terrorists' activities. On November 3, 2003, Israel's deputy UN ambassador, Arye Merkel, addressed the General Assembly to condemn UNRWA for its support of terrorism, pointing out that:

- In November 2002, Palestinian terrorists repeatedly fired on an Israeli military position in Gaza from the grounds of a UNRWA school while schoolchildren were there.

- In February 2003, Sama Bani Oudeh, an arrested Hamas operative, admitted that he had concealed explosives at a UNRWA school.
- Another Hamas operative, Nidal Abd el Fatah Abdullah Nazal, who worked as a UNRWA ambulance driver, admitted that he used the ambulance to ferry arms to terrorists and to pass operational orders among Hamas terrorists.
- Nahed Rashid Ahmed Attallah, a senior UNRWA employee in Gaza responsible for the distribution of assistance to refugees, admitted that he was an operative of both the PFLP and al-Fatah. He also admitted that he had used his UNRWA vehicle to help transport terrorists to attack Israeli soldiers and civilians. Nahed also used the vehicle to transport explosives to his brother-in-law Amer Karmout, an operative of the Palestinian Popular Resistance terrorist group.[21]

Because UNRWA does nothing to stop the terrorists, and because the Israelis do not search UN vehicles, UNRWA effectively helps the terrorists do their bloody work.

In my interview with Ziad abu Ziad, I asked him where the Palestinian Authority gets its funding, and he declined to answer. Later, I asked Ambassador Ayalon how much money is sent into the territories, and where it goes. Ayalon told me, "Since Arafat came to the Palestinian territories, they have received more than $5 billion in international aid. Per capita, that is more than the Europeans received after World War II," under the Marshall Plan.

So where does the money go? No one really knows, but, as Ambassador Ayalon pointed out, Arafat's personal wealth ranks him as the sixth wealthiest despot in the world.

The fact is that if the money being poured into the Palestinian areas were used for the benefit of the Palestinian people—instead of to support terror and to fill the pockets of Palestinian leaders—the West Bank and Gaza would look like Beverly Hills, not the ancient bullet-scarred shantytowns they now are. And the United Nations does nothing to hold Arafat accountable.

The UN preaches loudly that every state should fight against terrorism, but what does it do? It routinely cooperates with terrorists. The High Commission for Refugees, for example, lists dozens of NGO "donors and partners." According to a previously undisclosed CIA report drafted in 1998, some of these NGOs are known to be connected to terrorist organizations.

According to the CIA report:

> [N]early one-third of the Islamic NGOs in the Balkans have facilitated the activities of Islamic groups that engage in terrorism, including the Egyptian Al-Gama 'at al-Islamiyya, Palestinian Hamas, Algerian groups, and Lebanese Hizballah. Some of the terrorist groups such as al-Gama at al'Islamiyya have access to credentials for the UN High Commission for Refugees and other UN staffs in the former Yugoslavia.[22]

The CIA report mentions two High Commission "donors and partners" of particular interest: Human Appeal International, which has engaged in fund-raising for Hamas, and the Islamic Relief Agency, which ran guns in Bosnia, and, according to the CIA report, was controlled by Sudan's National Islamic Front.

What legitimacy does the UN have in the War on Terror? None.

CHAPTER THREE

"KOFIGATE":
THE UN OIL-FOR-FOOD PROGRAM

"Never has there been a financial rip-off of the magnitude of the UN oil-for-food scandal."

—Syndicated columnist William Safire

THERE IS MORE THAN ENOUGH EVIDENCE TO CONCLUDE THAT THE UN Oil-for-Food program—and the UN officials who ran it—provided Saddam Hussein with the means to bribe politicians, to deprive his people of needed food and medicine, and to literally steal billions of dollars. There is even emerging evidence that money from the program might have gone to support al-Qaeda.[1] Compared to the UN, Enron and WorldCom are models of corporate probity.

The Oil-for-Food program was created in 1995 by Security Council Resolution 986 to "provide for the humanitarian needs of the Iraqi people," while Iraq was otherwise embargoed, until it fulfilled Security Council resolutions requiring its disarmament.[2] To achieve this humanitarian goal, the Security Council allowed "the import of petroleum and petroleum products originating in Iraq, including financial and other essential transactions directly relating thereto, sufficient to produce a sum not exceeding a total of one billion United States dollars every ninety days."[3]

The resolution required "transparency" for each transaction, which meant that Iraq's oil exports, the buyers' oil imports, and their financial transactions would be under UN supervision and documentation for later audit. Payments were to be made into a special escrow account established by Kofi Annan.

The UN's share of the money was to be limited to covering the expenses of the program itself, the expenses of the UN weapons inspectors, and paying for the food and humanitarian aid that would be distributed to the Iraqi people.[4] To cover these costs, the UN was allowed to take a fee of 2.2 percent of the oil sales. But evidence shows that the UN might have taken, and allowed Saddam to take, much more. The UN was acting as a fiduciary for the Iraqi people, holding that money in trust for them. That trust was violated in ways that if the UN program managers had been officers of a U.S. corporation, they would be on their way to jail.

The Oil-for-Food program was the biggest financial program ever handled by the UN. And it was the most corrupt—at least so far. In the eight years of its existence, the UN claims the Oil-for-Food program resulted in the export of 3.4 billion barrels of oil, with 72 percent of the revenue allegedly going to humanitarian needs.[5] But much of the oil revenues apparently went to line the pockets of UN officials— possibly including Kofi Annan—and politicians around the world. The way the program was run demonstrates the depth of the scandal, and the urgent need for an investigation in which the UN isn't left to investigate itself.

On March 8, 2004, Michael Soussan, a former Oil-for-Food program coordinator for the UN, wrote in the *Wall Street Journal*:

> Were UN employees supposed to oppose Security Council resolutions, lobby for a lifting of sanctions and whitewash

the regime? That is what a majority of our Baghdad staff did. No one took action to redress their behavior.

The small minority who sought to hold the regime accountable were overruled, sidelined and sometimes branded spies by our own leadership. Meanwhile, the Saddam regime had infiltrated our mission in Iraq. All of the 4,233 local staff hired by the UN were required to report to Iraqi intelligence services. At our Baghdad HQ, UN mission leaders saw no problem with assigning Iraqi staff to man our switchboard, fax machines and photocopy room. Our 151 international observers were under siege, spied on by their employees and sometimes threatened by Iraqi officials when they tried to communicate information to New York that was embarrassing to the regime. All of this severely curtailed the UN's ability to do its job.[6]

The UN, in other words, allowed its operation to be infiltrated and used by Iraqi intelligence. Worse, the food and medical supplies the Iraqis bought with UN money were sold at inflated prices so Saddam Hussein could pocket the margin. Often the food and medicine was unfit for use. As Soussan reported:

[A]ccording to Security Council resolutions, the UN had a legal responsibility to report on any issue affecting the "adequacy, equitability and effectiveness" of the Oil-for-Food Program. Saddam's kickbacks affected all three aspects. There were many instances in the time I was there when the UN preferred to look the other way rather than address obvious signs of what was going wrong.

Take the medical sector. The regime's decision to use kickback-friendly front companies to purchase drugs meant that hospitals often received medicines that were nearly expired or otherwise damaged from unscrupulous suppliers. Iraqi

doctors would complain about the quality of the drug supply to our UN observers. Kurdish leaders raised similar con-
cerns directly with high-level UN officials. We knew exactly
how much the Iraqi government paid for any contract, and
we had the authority to inspect each shipment when it
crossed into Iraq. We had all the elements necessary to piece
together a clear picture of what was going on and alert the
Security Council to the fact that Saddam and his cronies
were buying poor quality products at inflated prices and
cashing in the difference. While the UN likes to claim this
was the most audited program in its history, I never once
read an audit report that raised questions about these practices—even though they were an open secret to anyone
involved in the program.[7]

The Iraqi Governing Council, which is building the new democratic
Iraq, has hired the Roland Berger Strategy Consultants firm to advise
it about, among other things, the Oil-for-Food program. After an ini-
tial investigation, Claude Hankes-Drielsma, chairman of UK operations
for Roland Berger, saw immediately that the Oil-for-Food program was
riddled with corruption.

In an urgent letter to UN secretary-general Kofi Annan dated
December 5, 2003, Hankes-Drielsma asked for an independent review
of the program:

> As a result of my findings here, combined with earlier infor-
> mation, I most strongly urge the UN to consider appointing
> an independent commission to review and investigate the
> 'Oil-for-Food Programme.' . . . My belief is that serious trans-
> gressions have taken place and may still be taking place.
>
> A further issue which needs most serious consideration
> and on which I would welcome an early discussion with you
> is how any debt which might have been incurred by Iraq

post–UN sanctions or made to rogue nations should be treated.

I spoke to Hankes-Drielsma on February 18, 2004. He had received no answer from Annan. But he had written another letter, this time to Hans Corell, the UN undersecretary for legal affairs and legal counsel. In that letter, Hankes-Drielsma specified the terms of the urgently needed investigation:

1. Oil-for-Food Program:
a. Indications are that not less than 10% was added to the value of all invoices to provide cash to Saddam Hussein (as much as $4 billion). If so, why was this not identified and prevented? Was the UN alerted to this at any stage? What action was taken and who was made aware of this allegation?
b. The UN received a fee of 2% of the value of all transactions to administer the program (as much as $1.1 billion US dollars.) What method was put in place by the UN to insure inspection of the quality of the food?
c. What controls were in place to monitor BNP [the bank of France] who handled the bulk of the [letters of credit], the total value of which may have [been] in the region of $47 billion US dollars?
d. The role of Jordanian Banks such as Jordan National Bank, Arab Bank and Housing Bank: Have there been a proper independent audit of all transactions and a proper accounting of all funds? Are these banks still holding funds, if so how much, why and how is this monitored? Was there a link between these banks and the Iraq Secret Service or any other part of the Saddam Hussein system?
e. Who at the UN carried overall responsibility for the Oil-for-Food program? Could there have been any link, directly or indirectly, with Saddam Hussein or middle men?

2. UN approval of Oil contracts under the [oil for food] program

a. Why did the UN approve oil contracts to non-end users? And without knowing the price?

b. A list of some of these contracts has been published by an Arab News Paper (this list which is known to me). It demonstrates beyond any doubt that Saddam Hussein bought political and other support under the aegis of the UN. In this list a "Mr. Sevan" is shown as receiving crude oil by this method through Panama.

c. VERY SIGNIFICANT SUPPLIES OF CRUDE OIL MADE TO NON-END USERS WERE TO OR TO THOSE LINKED TO INDIVIDUALS WITH POLITICAL INFLUENCE IN MANY COUNTRIES INCLUDING FRANCE AND JORDAN. WHAT METHOD OF CONTROL AND TRANSPARENCY OVER THESE SALES DID THE UN REQUIRE? [emphasis in original]

As of February 18, 2004, the UN was stonewalling. It issued a statement that said, in part:

> It is thus entirely possible, indeed probable, that Saddam Hussein's regime used loopholes in the Security Council's resolutions and operating framework for the Oil-for-Food Program to extract illicit funds from both purchasers and suppliers. However, these funds did not pass through the UN. The program itself was managed strictly within the mandate given to it by the Security Council and was subject to nearly 100 different audits, external and internal, between 1998 and 2003 and, as the secretary-general has said, this produced no evidence of any wrongdoing by any UN official.[8]

The UN was trying to have it both ways. On one hand, it admitted that the Iraqi regime used the cover of the UN program to buy influence around the world, and possibly in the UN itself. On the other, the

UN demanded that the world simply take its word that the program was completely free of abuse and corruption, based on its own "audits." The UN was refusing access to its documentation and the individuals who ran the program.

But even with the UN stonewalling, Hankes-Drielsma was able to make some important findings. I asked him which countries had clearly traded illegally with Iraq when the UN sanctions prohibiting trade were in place. He was sure of only one: France. (He later told the press that Russia had also benefited from corruption in the Oil-for-Food program.)

One likely reason the UN wouldn't allow any open review of the Oil-for-Food program is that it would reveal that UN officials were on Saddam's payroll. The list Hankes-Drielsma referred to was published in January 2004 in the Iraqi newspaper *al-Mada*. The *al-Mada* list includes both people and nations who were receiving bribes from the Iraqi regime, in the form of oil allocations below market price, which could then be sold on the world market. Along with several nations—France and Russia among them—was the name Hankes-Drielsma referred to in his letter: "Mr. Sevan," listed under Panama, implying that there were payments into an account in that nation.[9] The head of the Oil-for-Food program since 1997 was Benon Sevan, UN assistant secretary-general.

Others on *al-Mada*'s long list of bribed individuals, entities, and countries, include:

- Russia, which, through various entities, received about 1.4 *billion* barrels of oil
- British politician George Galloway, a longtime pro-Saddam voice
- Indonesian president Megawati Sukarnoputri
- Canadian oil executive Arthur Millholland
- The foreign minister of Chad
- Eleven French individuals and companies

The evidence is growing that the UN Oil-for-Food program might have robbed tens of billions of dollars from the people of Iraq, and paid it to the friends of Saddam Hussein, who, in turn, agitated against America's policy of regime change in Iraq.

We don't know how many—or which—leading UN officials were bribed, because the UN will not reveal its financial accounts. In late March 2004, the UN tried to placate its critics with an internal investigation, but as Hankes-Drielsma told me, only an independent investigation can have any credibility. The Iraqi Governing Council agreed, hiring KPMG Peat Marwick, an American accounting firm, and Freshfields Bruckhaus Deringer, a British law firm, to investigate the program.

UN recalcitrance appeared to change on April 21, 2004, when Kofi Annan appointed an "independent" panel to investigate the Oil-for-Food scandal and the Security Council unanimously passed a new resolution "welcoming" it.[10] The panel is composed of Paul Volcker, former chairman of the U.S. Federal Reserve; Mark Pieth, a Swiss money laundering expert; and Richard Goldstone, a South African war crimes prosecutor; and all UN members were called upon to cooperate fully. But this investigation, which will use UN staff and offices, and won't have the power to compel cooperation from the citizens or banks of any nation, isn't likely to get to the bottom of the scandal.

Most of the money from the program passed through French banks, and several sources have told me that some of the money was siphoned off to bribe high-ranking French politicians, possibly including President Jacques Chirac. French banks handled nearly $50 billion in Oil-for-Food transactions, and anyone who believes the French—or the Russians, the Germans, the Jordanians, the Syrians, and the rest—will be forthcoming with documentation and witnesses essential to the investigation is dreaming. Thus, it will be impossible for the Annan-appointed investigators to uncover the evidence necessary to reveal the wrongdoing of the UN, or many of its culpable members and staff.

The UN is now setting itself up to loot Iraq again. Hankes-Drielsma told me that the new "Iraq Development Fund" the UN will administer will probably suffer from the same corruption as the Oil-for-Food program did. The United States and those few Security Council members interested in seeing Iraq rebuilt rather than looted by the UN have little time to ensure that the new fund is administered honestly—outside of UN control and auditing. The Volcker investigation is no proof that the UN can police itself, because it is hobbled by the lack of authority to subpoena witnesses or documents from people, businesses, and governments that decide not to cooperate. As always, the UN's credibility depends on the honesty of its members and staff. However, honesty is not a commodity in great supply at the UN.

CHAPTER FOUR

QUAGMIRE DIPLOMACY

"As a matter of common sense and self-defense,
America will act against such emerging [terrorist] threats
before they are fully formed. We cannot defend America
and our friends by hoping for the best."

—2002 National Security Strategy of the United States

FOR MORE THAN FIVE MONTHS, AMERICA DELAYED THE MILITARY OPER-
ations in Iraq while the UN debated. The insurgency in Iraq that is now
claiming lives of American and allied soldiers—and will do so for
months or years to come—was planned in those months. Not just in
Iraq, but in Iran, Syria, Egypt, and Saudi Arabia.

Beginning in November 2002 and continuing through mid-March
2003, the Iraqis hid weapons and money and organized cells of insurgents throughout their strongholds. More weapons were bought—some
from France and Russia—and smuggled in. Insurgents from other
nations—Jordanians, Syrians, Iranians, Sudanese and many others—
came in to fight against the freedom and democracy the United States
is trying to give Iraq. How many lives could have been spared had we
acted more quickly? Would we have caught Saddam with his weapons
of mass destruction (WMD) if we'd acted sooner?

In December 2002, Iraq reportedly began moving its WMD—its weapons, research and manufacturing equipment, records, and personnel—out of Iraq to Syria and Lebanon.[1] Right up to the beginning of the military campaign, people and materials were being moved into Syria on the highway from Baghdad through the border city of al-Qaim. After the Iraqi regime fell, the legitimacy of the war was called into question by Kofi Annan, French president Jacques Chirac, and many others who wanted to prove that the American action was illegal aggression because no WMD had been found.

America's *casus belli* was threefold: Iraq's WMD program, its connections to terrorism, and Saddam Hussein's oppression of the Iraqi people. But the principal justification for war was Saddam's WMD program, because it was a violation of the Gulf War cease-fire and UN resolution, as well as a serious threat to world peace. But now that American troops have failed to find WMD in Iraq, this justification has been, in the eyes of many, proven false. Though Saddam was hip-deep in terrorism, so are other nations in the Middle East and elsewhere. Why should America have singled out Iraq?

The better question is, why, if the president was convinced military action was essential, did he fail to go to war when the time was right?

While President George W. Bush readied the best-telegraphed military punch in American history, Saddam and his allies were acting. With regard to WMD, Deputy Secretary of Defense Paul Wolfowitz told me, "One possible area where they might have used that time is if they moved stuff to Syria, or buried stuff or otherwise hid stuff. We certainly know—I think [WMD search chief] David Kay has confirmed this—as Powell said in his February [2003] speech to the UN that they were...hiding things. And they were doing this most actively in the period after the resolutions....Evidence suggests that they were still cleaning things up after the war began, and even after the fall of Baghdad."

As soon as military action began, many of the top members of Saddam's regime fled to Syria, some used Syria as a transit point to other nations, and some even returned to Iraq. America underestimated the complicity and recklessness of the Syrian regime. Bashar Assad was convinced that America wouldn't attack Syria—and he was right.

I asked Paul Wolfowitz if Saddam gained military advantage because of the endless UN proceedings. He said, "I think relatively little. Because, maybe, Saddam never believed we would actually act. If that's the case—and I underline 'if that's the case' because we're really speculating here, wildly—one interpretation is that we may have some members of the Security Council to thank for that. And there is even a little bit of evidence of that point among the comments that have been made by some of the 'black list' people when they've been interviewed that suggests that they were convinced that the French would bail them out." (The "black list" people are those high in the Saddam regime who have been captured.)

Nevertheless, the cost of the UN delay is the time it gave Saddam and the terrorist neighbors of Iraq to plan the postwar insurgency and to move or hide WMD. At the beginning of 2004, President Bush was faced with a reelection campaign that was vastly more complicated by the apparent failure to find WMD stockpiles. More importantly, the failure to find WMD in Iraq hurt America's standing all over the world, but especially in the Arab countries, and gave critics an effective political weapon against America. Government-controlled media, such as Saudi Arabia's *Arab News*, are relentlessly critical of America generally and President Bush individually. The theory that Bush led America into an unnecessary war has become an accepted fact to the UN, to much of Europe, and, of course, to the Democratic Party of John Kerry.

The fact is that there is still no explanation of Iraq's WMD program, what form weapons might have been in (deployable weapons or merely research programs), or what had happened to them. The delay put on our military operation by the president's courting of the UN has hugely complicated the solving of that mystery.

Around 500 B.C., Chinese military philosopher Sun Tzu wrote that surprise and deception are two key principles of strategy.[2] In a war against terrorists and terrorist nations, surprise and deception are even more important. It was certain—even before Colin Powell's presentation to the General Assembly in February—that the UN would not act. But for yet another month, we stayed our hand while the UN kabuki dance played on.

In Afghanistan, America succeeded in destroying the Taliban regime and the terrorist infrastructure—training camps and safe havens— that enabled terrorists to mount large-scale attacks. In Iraq, American forces defeated the Iraqi army, but the other necessary level of success—capturing and destroying Iraq's WMD—required surprise. UN diplomacy and preemption cannot coexist. We have to choose one or the other. If the subordination of U.S. war plans to UN diplomacy is repeated, it will be fatal to George W. Bush's strategy of preempting terrorist attacks by military action.

The diplomatic delay to the Iraq War was costly in the most important sense: in blood. Intelligence sources said—all through the period of quagmire diplomacy—that terrorists from other nations were slipping into Iraq, and that Iraq was receiving military supplies from nations—France and Russia—that were supposedly supporting UN diplomacy. And the Iraqis were given time to plan an insurgency, in coordination with the terrorists.

That insurgency went into action almost as soon as the Saddam statue was toppled in Firdos Square in Baghdad, and continues. As of February 10, 2004, more than 530 Americans had died in Iraq, more than half of them after May 1, 2003, when the major military action in Iraq was declared over.[3] How many of these lives were lost because the Iraqis and the terrorists had been given time to plan their insurgency is unknowable, as is how many lives would have been spared had the diplomatic effort been shortened. But the point is the same: Subordinating military action to diplomacy in preemptive war cannot work.

Preemption of terrorist threats is essential to preventing future terrorist attacks such as those of September 11, 2001. Preemptive action does not have to be unilateral. Diplomacy—outside the UN, forging other "coalitions of the willing"—can precede military action. But it can be done only in secret, involving allies in military plans before attacks are carried out. That sort of diplomacy—linked closely to the decision to preempt, and integrated into military planning—can help avoid the principal failure of the Iraq campaign: the failure to prevent the terrorist nation from arranging for its most important assets to escape the preemptive strike. Deception is as much a part of diplomacy as secrecy and surprise are parts of war-making.

The damage of the UN-imposed delay will last for decades. If we do not find Saddam's WMD, America will be branded an unjustified aggressor that lied its way into war, and few nations—even our closest allies, such as Britain—will join us in another military campaign. Because the UN will not change, we cannot again step into its quagmire of diplomacy.

CHAPTER FIVE

SECRETARY-GENERAL KOFI ANNAN: A SYMPTOM OF THE UN DISEASE

"I admire the martial and commanding air with which the right honorable gentleman treats the facts. He stands no nonsense from them."

—Winston Churchill, speaking of a parliamentary foe

IN 1997, KOFI ANNAN OF GHANA BEGAN HIS FIRST TERM AS SECRETARY-general. These days, we are used to seeing Annan walking down lines of blue-bereted UN troops, reviewing them as though he were their commander in chief. It is by assumption of that role—completely unjustified by the UN Charter, but encouraged by France, Germany, Russia, and others, including America's Democratic Party—that the UN secretary-general has been transformed from an administrative officer into someone with the pretension and grandiosity of a head of state.

Kofi Annan is the most activist secretary-general—at least in a self-serving sense—the UN has ever had. Rather than encouraging members to deal with international crises, he has sought to expand the UN's prominence and influence for its own sake.

"So yeah, I'm still pretty much for the UN. I still think Kofi Annan's a good guy who deserved the Nobel Peace Prize." This was former president

Bill Clinton's assessment (in April 2003) of the man who—on Clinton's watch—became not only the pal of Saddam Hussein, but worked to thwart action against terrorists and the nations that support them.

Richard Butler was the head of the UN special commission (UNSCOM) charged with ensuring that Saddam had disarmed Iraq of WMD. He began his book about his years in UNSCOM by writing:

> The greatest threat to life on earth is weapons of mass destruction—nuclear, chemical, biological. These weapons do not exist in nature. They have been made by man, generally as the result of sophisticated research, and complex, costly processes.
>
> The community of nations has recognized this threat; indeed, perhaps the most important achievement in the second half of the twentieth century was the weaving of a tapestry of treaties designed to contain and then eliminate it. This work was never easy, and its implementation has been challenged repeatedly. The most determined and diabolical of such challenges has been mounted by the dictator of Iraq—Saddam Hussein.
>
> For almost two decades, he has sought to acquire these weapons and the means of their delivery. In most cases, he has been successful and even took the further step of using them. . . . He shares with Adolf Hitler the infamy of having used chemicals for genocidal purposes.[1]

Butler's job was tough enough, but Kofi Annan's personal interference made the job impossible.

UN Security Council Resolution 687 stated the terms of the cease-fire of the first Gulf War. It required that Saddam:

> Shall accept unconditionally the destruction, removal or rendering harmless, under international supervision, of: (a) all

chemical and biological weapons and all stocks of agents
and related subsystems and components and all research,
development, support and manufacturing facilities related
thereto; and (b) all ballistic missiles with a range greater
than one hundred and fifty kilometers, and all related major
parts and repair and production facilities.[2]

Violation of the terms of the cease-fire, by any reading of international law, meant that a state of war again existed. But Kofi Annan
didn't see it that way. For him, the cease-fire was forever negotiable,
regardless of continued Iraqi violations.

By 1998, the UN Security Council had passed six resolutions requiring Saddam to disarm, and he had failed to comply with every one of
them. American and British pilots, enforcing the "no-fly" zones, from
which Iraqi aircraft were prohibited entry, faced almost daily ground
fire and surface-to-air missile attack by the Iraqis. UNSCOM weapons
inspectors were denied entry to the hundred or so "presidential sites"
that were prime locations to discover WMD. Many of these sites—
some of them ten or fifteen square miles in size and including almost
one hundred buildings—were known to conceal extensive underground
complexes. A cacophony of intelligence reports about WMD activities
at these sites—some from Iraqi National Congress sources in Iraq—
poured in.[3]

Saddam demanded "modalities"—written procedures regarding
how inspections would be conducted—before allowing Butler's
UNSCOM inspectors access to the presidential palaces and other sites.
Those "modalities"—first established in 1996—hampered UNSCOM's
ability to conduct no-notice inspections, and limited access to too many
sites for the inspectors' job to be done properly.[4]

Annan sided with the Iraqis, thus tabling any hope of the inspections
succeeding. Butler was forced to accept a Russian and a Frenchman on
his staff, who of course acted as agents of their governments, which dis-
approved of intrusive UNSCOM inspections.[5]

The UN Charter, in uncharacteristically clear and strong language, requires that the staff of the secretary-general be independent of instruction from individual governments, and member governments agree to not seek to influence them.[6] This rule has never been followed. Ambassador Jose Sorzano, who served as Jeane Kirkpatrick's UN deputy during the Reagan administration, told me that the Soviet Union consistently broke the rule. Richard Butler also found this to be an "empty rule" while heading UNSCOM.[7] But Butler's biggest problem wasn't with the staff. It was with the secretary-general himself.

In February 1998, Annan flew to Baghdad. He went without instructions from the Security Council and without any authority to negotiate away the terms of the cease-fire resolution.[8] But that's exactly what he did.

In several meetings, at one of which he was photographed bowing to Saddam Hussein,[9] Annan made an agreement reinstituting the "modalities" Butler had fought so hard to eliminate, and agreed to other "special procedures" that fettered the inspections of Saddam's palaces.[10] After Annan sold out the inspectors, the Security Council ratified the Annan agreement, with the Clinton administration's approval. As Butler saw it, "I had no illusions about what had happened—UNSCOM's mandate had, at least in part, been bargained away in Baghdad."[11]

In the end, Saddam kicked UNSCOM out of Iraq in August 1998, declaring its work done. Once again, Annan and his staff—with the help of the French and the Russians—stepped in to advocate a "comprehensive review" of the Iraqi disarmament, which was completed two months later. The report concluded that Iraq had not complied with its obligations and that sanctions should stay in place. Saddam responded by rejecting any cooperation with UNSCOM, and demanded that Butler be removed as chairman.[12]

American and British military forces eventually compelled Saddam to agree to let UNSCOM inspectors resume their efforts on November 15, 1998. But once again, the Iraqis denied them access to crucial sites. So on December 16, 1998, American and British aircraft—as well as about two hundred cruise missiles—began hitting military targets in Iraq to force Saddam to comply.

Three days later, President Clinton addressed the nation, telling us that the "seventy-hour" strategy had worked and that Saddam's WMD programs had been degraded.[13] But in fact, though British and American jets had bombed almost one hundred targets, Saddam had not bound himself to any verifiable disarmament, and the Clinton administration had shown yet again that it was satisfied with spin rather than substance. As the victors of the Gulf War, the British and Americans had every right to enforce the cease-fire agreement requiring Iraq's disarmament independently of the United Nations. But the Clinton administration never took that decisive action.

Another UN inspection team was formed. It was called UNMOVIC: the UN Monitoring, Verification, and Inspection Commission. Its head, Hans Blix, was a Swedish diplomat who was far less aggressive than Richard Butler and became a vocal opponent of the war with Iraq.

On January 14, 2003, Annan was asked about a statement by British foreign minister Jack Straw that Britain reserved the right to act militarily against Iraq without Security Council approval. Annan disagreed. "I think the Council discussions and the Council resolutions, which guide me, make it quite clear that they will have to go to the Council for further discussions, and for the Council—which has threatened serious consequences—I hope, to also determine what those consequences would be."[14]

On March 13, 2003, Annan was asked whether U.S. military action against Iraq, without Security Council approval, violated the UN Charter. He answered, "If the U.S. and others were to go outside the Council and take military action, it would not be in conformity with the Charter."[15]

But if the Iraq campaign was a violation of the UN Charter, then so was the Afghanistan campaign, which was undertaken without UN permission, and so were France's military interventions in the Ivory

Coast and the Central African Republic in 2003. Moreover, if, by Kofi Annan's thinking, the U.S. was in violation of the UN Charter, it was also acting in violation of international law.

Annan and the UN General Assembly are silent about the most egregious violations of the UN Charter regarding terrorism. Syria and Iran, for example, are members in good standing. But Kofi Annan and the UN would like to create a legal shackle on United States foreign policy by means of the International Criminal Court.

Kofi's Court

The International Criminal Court (ICC) was created by the Rome Statute to have universal jurisdiction over war crimes and crimes against humanity.[16] Universal jurisdiction is something new—and dangerous. The ICC has expanded the definition of "war crimes" far beyond that established by the Geneva Convention. Among the new definitions are "environmental crimes" and attacks that might cause incidental loss of life.[17] Careful where you pitch that tent, soldier. Don't disturb that spotted owl nesting in the tree above you. And don't even think of bombing that building where your enemy has his headquarters. The enemy is smart enough to have set up camp with protected wetlands to one side and an endangered species to the other. The Rome Statute has even made it possible to prosecute as "war criminals" U.S. soldiers who take terrorists prisoner and isolate them—as at Guantanamo Bay, Cuba—for interrogation. Bill Clinton signed the treaty implementing the ICC on December 31, 2000, but did not submit it for Senate ratification. In other words, he tried, extra-legally, to bind the United States to the UN's latest power grab.

And a power grab it clearly was. Under one reading of the ICC law, not only soldiers and generals, but presidents and Cabinet ministers could be punished by the International Criminal Court for war crimes and for violating UN resolutions. As former secretary of state Henry Kissinger pointed out, in its current form the ICC represents a fundamental assault on American sovereignty, rights, and practices under the Constitution.[18]

Kissinger writes:

> Distrusting national governments, many of the advocates of
> universal jurisdiction seek to place politicians under the
> supervision of magistrates and the judicial system. But pros-
> ecutorial discretion without accountability is precisely one
> of the flaws of the International Criminal Court. Definitions
> of relevant crimes are vague and highly susceptible to politi-
> cized application. Defendants will not enjoy due process as
> understood in the United States. Any signatory state has the
> right to trigger an investigation. As the US experience with
> special prosecutors investigating the executive branch
> shows, such a procedure is likely to develop its own momen-
> tum without time limits and can turn into an instrument of
> political warfare.[19]

President George W. Bush has rightly rejected the ICC treaty, and
took the trouble to negotiate immunity for U.S. forces serving as UN
peacekeepers, ensuring that the ICC could not prosecute them. Kofi
Annan opposed him, and in June 2003, addressed the Security Council before it voted on whether to extend—by one year—that immunity.
Annan said approving immunity from ICC prosecution would undermine the "legitimacy" of peacekeeping. He criticized the United States
for giving the impression that "it wished to claim an absolute and permanent immunity for people serving in the operations [the Security
Council] establishes."[20] Annan lobbied hard against America's position,
and lost. The fight will recur as long as the ICC is in existence, or until
America ceases to participate in UN peacekeeping missions.

The ICC is finding other ways to expand its power. One of these is
broadening the Geneva Convention's limited definition of prohibited
weapons. Under the Convention, poison gas and biological warfare are
outlawed. Cluster bombs—which dispense hundreds of small bombs
over a target area—are highly effective against concentrations of
troops, and some have the capability to destroy armored vehicles as

well.[21] At this writing, seven academics are bringing a case against British use of cluster bombs in the 2003 Iraq campaign, and the ICC has launched an investigation that might result in war crime indictments against British commanders, even against Prime Minister Tony Blair.[22] Included in the investigation is the use of bunker-busting bombs that penetrate and destroy underground targets. A group calling itself "Peacerights" wants to have the ICC declare the Iraq campaign itself illegal. One of its lawyers, Professor Bill Bowring of London Metropolitan University, said, "The U.S. cannot be tried before the court because it refuses to sign up to [the ICC treaty]. The UK did."[23] Just so.

Meanwhile, George W. Bush has repeatedly invited the UN to help rebuild Iraq, but Kofi Annan has resisted cooperation with the United States, because the UN would not have full control of the effort. "I need to weigh the degree of risk that the UN is being asked to accept against the substance of the role we are being asked to fulfill," he said.[24]

Annan misses no chance to assert the UN's power. When Saddam Hussein was captured on December 13, 2003, Annan promptly declared that Hussein should not be sentenced to the death penalty in any trial. "The UN does not support the death penalty," he said. "In all the courts we have set up [UN officials] have not included death penalty."[25] That a sovereign government of Iraq might execute Saddam in accordance with its own laws is irrelevant to the secretary-general. To him, only the UN should rule.

The Legitimacy Scam

"Colin in Kofi Land" was the headline of a *Wall Street Journal* editorial on October 13, 2003, which made two very important points. First:

> The apparent failure of the U.S. push for another UN resolution on Iraq is at least a clarifying moment. A body incapable of agreeing to endorse even post facto reconstruction could certainly never have been expected to enforce its Iraq resolutions in the first place. So much for the argument that

a kinder, gentler approach by the Bush administration would have won UN support.[26]

That proposed resolution, which didn't give the French and Germans the control of post-Saddam Iraq they demanded, proved redundantly that the Security Council had ceased to perform its principal duty: to deal with threats to peace. But the second point was even more important:

UN Secretary General Kofi Annan has made it clear that he's now more interested in defeating President Bush than he ever was in toppling Saddam Hussein. Mr. Annan knows that Mr. Bush's policy... poses a serious challenge to what he claims is the "unique legitimacy" of the collection of despots he leads—indeed to the legitimacy of the unaccountable Secretary General himself.[27]

Annan realizes that any time the United States acts without first getting permission of the UN Security Council, it reduces the power and influence of the UN, and thus his own power and influence. In setting the agenda for his "reform" panel, Annan planned to deal thusly with the American threat to UN power:

I have tried to work with the Members to find ways of improving our Organization to make it more effective, and in fact also of trying to develop international law, because some of the questions that the panel will have to deal with touch on not just structures and process of the United Nations, but how the international community organizes to cooperate and organizes itself to ensure that we maintain peace and security. And it really is pushing the development of international law where they will have to discuss questions of when preventive war is acceptable, under what rules and who approves.[28]

"Under what rules, and who approves." That's the only issue in Annan's mind, and in the minds of the UN's most faithful supporters. Annan is more interested in increasing the UN's power to control American action than he is in doing the job for which he was hired. Kofi Annan and Jacques Chirac see the UN—as do too many others, including the leaders of the Democratic Party—as a brake on America's drive to preempt the terrorist threats it faces. Who approves preemptive action, the UN or the United States acting as a sovereign nation in accordance with our Constitution? That's the only issue for the UN's supporters, for the American people, and for our president.

The legitimacy of Annan's actions—of every UN action—derives from UN member states' legitimacy. International consensus can grant legitimacy, but only if that consensus comes from free nations. The Warsaw Pact always had a consensus among its members, because those "members" had no choice. In treaties, nations make binding agreements that carry the legitimacy of international law. Whether Annan sprinkles UN holy water over something doesn't make it bad or good. Legitimacy in international affairs results from nations acting peacefully, in their political and economic interests, or militarily, to resist aggression and repel or preempt an attack. Facts give rise to legitimacy. The UN, as much as it might like to, cannot create or destroy such facts.

CHAPTER SIX

THE UN BUREAUCRACY: NICE WORK IF YOU CAN GET IT

*"Even though most staff join the UN out of support for the
ideals of the Organization, the UN still has difficulty in
attracting and retaining staff from countries with high pay
levels. If the UN wants to continue to attract highly qualified
and dedicated professionals, it must be a competitive
employer offering attractive conditions."*

—UN website

AMERICAN TAXPAYERS SPEND MORE ON THE UN THAN THEY KNOW, because while most people look at our UN dues, that's only about half the bill. The other half is made up of voluntary contributions and subsidiary dues. All told, in 2004 America will throw about $7 billion down the UN drain.

Ever since the UN was founded, the U.S. has been its biggest source of funds. Under the UN's scale of assessments, the United States now pays a maximum of 22 percent of the entire UN's "regular" budget, while some forty-six nations are asked to pay only the minimum—0.001 percent[1]—and some fail to pay altogether. In 2003, the assessed dues for the regular UN—not counting the other dues and voluntary contributions—amounted to almost $3.5 billion.[2] Some large nations, Russia and China, for example, were assessed only $18.6 million and $23.7 million respectively in 2003.[3]

Not included in the basic UN assessment are the "voluntary" contributions America makes to a large number of UN programs.

Looking at the UN's mass of programs and activities—and its huge, overpaid bureaucracy—it's easy to see how the UN burns up all that money so quickly. What is not so easy to understand is why the budgetary reforms insisted on by the United States and other nations are not happening, except that Congress is so easily fooled by the UN.

For example, according to a 2003 study by the Congressional Research Service (CRS), reforms imposed by Kofi Annan are reducing the size of the UN bureaucracy.[4] Unfortunately, the CRS study is flat-out wrong.

In 1947, when Trygve Lie was the first secretary-general, the UN staff was about 1,200 strong.[5] According to the CRS report, Annan's "reforms" have cut the UN Secretariat's staff—which serves not just the office of the secretary-general but the myriad UN agencies around the world—from about twelve thousand employees to fewer than nine thousand today.[6] But, as the *Wall Street Journal* points out, "The staff of the Secretariat, the central bureaucracy that serves core UN agencies, is a patchwork of entrenched employees with permanent contracts and others with little job security." According to the UN's own website, and the *Journal*'s analysis of its data, the UN Secretariat staff hasn't been cut to nine thousand: It has grown to more than seventeen thousand. So much for Annan's reforms.

The increase has been concealed—at least from the supposedly probing eye of the Congressional Research Service—by shifting employees from permanent to non-permanent status. By increasing the numbers of non-permanent employees—employees whose job security now depends on the secretary-general's favor—Annan has created a bureaucracy to serve his own agenda.

By UN rule, staff salaries are among the highest in the world. The salaries are set in accordance with the "Noblemaire Principle," which, according to the UN, states that "the international civil service should be able to recruit staff from its Member states, including the highest-paid."[7]

Consider the salaries of many of those seventeen thousand UN bureaucrats:

- Thirty-six undersecretaries-general, each drawing a salary of $186,144, plus home leave and family visit travel expenses, rent subsidies, U.S. tax exemptions, expense accounts for entertainment, and various other perks
- Forty assistant secretaries-general, paid $169,366, plus similar perks
- 433 directors, paid between $126,713 and $154,223, plus perks
- 5,106 professionals, paid between $42,944 and $131,299 (yes, plus perks)
- 6,795 "general services" employees, paid between $30,147 and $80,232[8]

That adds up to about seventeen thousand UN bureaucrats pulling down a total of just shy of $1 billion. Nice work if you can get it. And you can, if you play the game.

ET Went Home, UN Bureaucrats Don't

There are 191 member nations of the UN General Assembly, and the vast majority of them are impoverished, bereft of every political and economic freedom Americans enjoy.[9] When their staff land in New York, they live in a free and luxurious world unlike anything they have ever experienced—or could experience—at home. They like it, and they want to stay. And because they want to stay, they work their way into the UN bureaucracy.

Slowly, over the years, bureaucrats from the Third World have taken over the UN staff. In 1946, only 20 percent of the UN Secretariat's staff was from Central and South America, Africa, the Middle East, and Central, East, and Southeast Asia. The remaining 80 percent were from North America and Europe.[10] During the Cold

Table 3. U.S. Voluntary Contributions
the Foreign Assistance Act (International Organ

	FY2001 Actual
UN Development Program (UNDP)	87
UN Children's Fund (UNICEF)[b]	109
World Food Program (WFP)	5
UN Development Fund for Women (UNIFEM)	1
International Contributions for Scientific, Educational, & Cultural Activities	1.8
WMO Voluntary Co-op Program	2
UN Environment Program (UNEP)	10
Montreal Protocol Multilateral Fund	26
International Conservation Programs[c] (CITES, ITTO, IUCN, Ramsar, CCD)	5.5
UN Voluntary Fund Torture Victims	5
Climate Stabilization Fund (IPCC, UNFCC)	6.5
ICAO Aviation Security Fund	.3
UN Voluntary Fund for Advisory Services & Technical Cooperation	1.5
IAEA Voluntary Programs[d]	50.5
UN Guards in Iraq	—
UN Population Fund (UNFPA)[e]	21.5
Reserved—To Be Allocated	—
Total	**333.6**

a) Does not include U.S. contributions to UN High Commissioner for Refugee (UNHCR) programs ($255 million in FY2002) and to UN Relief and Works Agency for Palestine Refugees in the Near East (UNRWA) ($119 million in FY2002), financed through the Migration and Refugee Assistance Account; World Food Program commodities donations; WHO Special Programs; UN Volunteers; and UN International Drug Control Program.

b) Appropriated under Child Survival Program.

to UN Programs Financed Through
izations and Programs) a(in millions of dollars)

FY2002 Actual	FY2003 Estimate	FY2004 Request
97	100	100
120	120	120
6	—	6
1	1	1
1.8	1.8	.5
2	2	2
10.8	10	10
25	23	21
7.7	6.2	6.2
5	5	5
7.4	5.6	5.6
.3	.3	1
1.5	1.5	1.5
49	50	50
—	—	.7
—	—	—
—	25	25
335.5	**351.4**	**355.5**

c) Only CITES is a UN program.

d) Requested and Appropriated under Non-Proliferation, Antiterrorism, Demining and Related Programs account.

e) Congress appropriated $34 million for FY2002, but the State Department determined that UNFPA was ineligible for the U.S. contribution. $34 million was appropriated for FY2003 provided that eligibility can be certified.

War, there was a pronounced shift in favor of Communist states. Former UN ambassador Jeane Kirkpatrick told me, "The Secretariat was then [in the 1980s] heavily infiltrated with Soviet personnel who were engaged in espionage activity. The Soviets and Cubans were both grossly overrepresented inside the Secretariat. That's changed now." By 2003, the problem wasn't Communist subversion, but Third World domination.

According to the *Wall Street Journal*'s summary of UN data on its staff, in 2003:

- 12 percent were from Central and South America
- 19 percent were from Africa
- 5 percent were from the Middle East or Central Asia
- 18 percent were from East and Southeast Asia

In sum, North American and Europe—the democratic West—is now in the minority, and more than half of the UN Secretariat's employees come from the Third World.[11] While the U.S. provides most of the money for the UN, the Third World provides most of the people who determine and implement the UN agenda.

"The Name of the Game Is the Game"

That's what former U.S. economic counselor Dennis Goodman said about the culture of the UN. Goodman, a career foreign service officer, spent six years butting his head against the UN bureaucracy. "They don't care whether they're talking about commodity prices or transnational corporations," he told me. Every resolution from ECOSOC—the UN's Economic and Social Council, for which he worked—had to end with the magic words: "The secretary-general should study this resolution and report back to ECOSOC," thus ensuring another round of meetings and more study. And longer job security for the bureaucrats. In essence, the UN has become an American-subsidized program to employ Third World bureaucrats. "They think the U.S. treasury is the common heritage of mankind," said Goodman. To that end, Third World countries sign treaties that cost them nothing, but can cost developed nations dearly. The Lebanese, for example, have signed on to all sorts of UN-generated treaties, such as Biodiversity, Climate Change, Desertification, Hazardous Wastes, Law of the Sea, Nuclear Test Ban, Ozone Layer Protection, Ship Pollution, and Wetlands.[12] All of these treaties put burdens on our economy, not Lebanon's.

Here's how America's taxpayer billions, in fiscal year 2004, will be spent at the UN:

United Nations	$340.7 (in millions)
UN War Crimes Tribunal	$30
Iraq War Crimes Commission	$2
Food and Agriculture Organization	$72.4
International Atomic Energy Agency	$54.3
International Civil Aviation Agency	$12.6
International Labor Organization	$50.4
International Maritime Organization	$1.2
International Telecommunications Union	$6.6
UN Educational, Scientific, and Cultural Organization	$71.5
Universal Postal Union	$1.3
World Health Organization	$93.6
World Intellectual Property Organization	$1
World Meteorological Organization	$8.3
TOTAL:	**$746 million**[13]

In truth, some of these agencies do the Lord's work. Do we want to immunize millions in Africa against smallpox? We did, and the World Health Organization did it. Some humanitarian UN agencies work well, but many do not.

One of the best examples is the UN Human Rights Commission (HRC), which the United States helped create in 1947. In May 2001, the U.S. was thrown off the Commission while Sudan—one of the few nations that allows slavery and is one of the worst abusers of human rights on the planet—was voted on. Libya was elected chair of the committee. Today, the HRC is composed of fifty-three members, including Communist China, Cuba, Sudan, Nigeria, Saudi Arabia, and Zimbabwe, among the most severe abusers of human rights in the world. And yet the United States has rejoined the HRC's membership, lending its good name to this farce. Why? Because it's the UN, that's why.

By participating in such UN forums, we contribute to the UN's spread of corruption and propaganda. If talk is cheap in America, it's altogether free at the UN. The UN document system enables every delegation to have its scribblings circulated as "official" UN documents.[14] Jose Sorzano, Jeane Kirkpatrick's deputy UN ambassador, wrote, "In this manner all sorts of propaganda are later distributed with the UN's imprimatur."[15] The UN corrupts debate by giving propaganda a dignity it could never otherwise have.

And what is our reward for consenting to this corruption? More bills, and an endless stream of proposed treaties, resolutions, and other claptrap designed to burden our economy and raid our treasury. At the end of 2002, the UN said we still owed it $12 million for "international tribunals" (not including the International Criminal Court), $535 million for peacekeeping missions (which is over and above the congressionally set cap of 25 percent of the entire UN peacekeeping budget), and $190 million in back dues.[16]

On November 22, 1999, Senator John Kerry wrote in the *Washington Times,* "When we fail to pay our U.N. dues, we undermine support from our friends and allies who stand by us in places such as Kosovo and Iraq." But the support of friends and allies can't be bought at the UN. It can be gained only by sharing values and goals. All too few of the UN's members share any of America's values, goals, or interest in preserving freedom.

CHAPTER SEVEN

THE UN'S FATAL FLAWS

"Far along the world-wide whisper of the south-wind rushing warm,
With the standards of the peoples plunging thro' the thunder-storm;
Till the war-drum throbb'd no longer, and the battle flags were furl'd
In the Parliament of man, the Federation of the world.
There the common sense of most shall hold a fretful realm in awe,
And the kindly earth shall slumber, lapt in universal law."

—Alfred, Lord Tennyson, "Locksley Hall"

IN THE ATLANTIC CHARTER OF JULY 1941, FRANKLIN DELANO ROOSEVELT and Winston Churchill framed, in rather wishful terms, their vision of a postwar world of peaceful, self-governing nations participating in "a wider and permanent system of general security," including disarmament.[1] In February 1942, representatives of twenty-six nations met in Washington and signed a "United Nations" declaration, pledging to fulfill the Atlantic Charter.[2] By the spring of 1943, the United States had a fairly complete draft of a UN charter, which had been shared with the British.[3]

In February 1945, months before Germany or Japan surrendered, the leaders of the major powers—America, Britain, and Russia—gathered at the Black Sea resort of Yalta to discuss the postwar world and outlined what would become the UN. From the start, pretending that Joseph

Stalin shared the goals of the Atlantic Charter was a farce. But there was another weasel in the woodpile: Charles de Gaulle, the very model of the modern pestilential Frenchman, whose pomposity earned the dislike of both Roosevelt and Churchill. At the Casablanca Conference in 1942, the British prime minister and American president met with de Gaulle.

> Brendan Bracken, who was in charge of Churchill's arrangements at the hectic three-day meetings, at one point vented his frustrations at his boss. Churchill replied, "Well, Brendan, you have only one cross to bear. I have a double cross—the double cross of Lorraine."
>
> "The general's problem," sympathized Bracken, "is that he thinks he is the reincarnation of Joan of Arc."
>
> "No, the problem is," concluded Churchill, "my bishops won't allow me to burn him."[4]

Roosevelt's dislike for de Gaulle, less eloquently expressed than Churchill's, nevertheless had a greater effect. Roosevelt excluded de Gaulle from the 1944 Dumbarton Oaks conference, at which the UN charter was further developed, and again from the Yalta summit at which the postwar world took shape. Because de Gaulle wasn't included in the summit, he reached a state of indignation that only the French can achieve, and which—as the president of the Free French nation—he shared with the rest of the Free French government.

The exclusion of France wasn't the result of a petty personality conflict. By no measure could post–World War II France be considered one of the world's great powers. Its crushed economy would take many years to recover. It had no significant army, air force, or navy. In short, France demanded recognition as a world power despite the fact that it clearly wasn't one.

Having been excluded from Yalta, de Gaulle at first turned down a permanent seat on the UN Security Council and said he would not send a French delegation to the final drafting conference in San Francisco.

But, as the conference grew near, de Gaulle changed his mind and agreed that France would be a sponsor of the conference.[5] To soothe de Gaulle's bruised ego, American secretary of state Edward Stettinius asked him to reconsider his rejection of the permanent Security Council seat, and de Gaulle consented.

By the time the San Francisco conference began in late April 1945, Roosevelt was dead and Harry Truman, who had been involved in the UN preparations since 1943,[6] was president. Truman was even more of a dreamer than Roosevelt had been. He had a favorite poem that had he recited from a very young age: Alfred, Lord Tennyson's "Locksley Hall."[7] The poem envisions a "parliament of man" ruling over a peaceful, untroubled world—something, unfortunately, that the UN would never be.

One of the greatest bones of contention in the San Francisco conference was the authority of the Security Council. Under the proposed UN charter, the General Assembly could do what it liked; no nation was bound by General Assembly resolutions. The Security Council was another matter. To overcome the perceived weakness of the former League of Nations, the new UN Security Council's resolutions were supposed to be binding on all member states.

The Soviets had been expelled from the League of Nations because of their attack on Finland in the early days of World War II. To ensure that Soviet Russia wasn't expelled from the UN, Stalin demanded a veto over Security Council resolutions, and he got it. When the San Francisco conference ended, the Security Council was structured with five permanent members and six non-permanent members that would be elected to two-year terms.[8] All five permanent members were given the veto. And, of course, one of the permanent members was France. Blame the State Department, blame the Russians, blame whomever you'd like, the result is the same: France and Soviet Russia held veto power over every crucial UN decision.

There are many defects in the UN Charter. Some of them made the failure of the organization inevitable:

- False equality among nations: Article 2 says, "The Organization is based on the principle of sovereign equality of all its Members." Equality among men—the foundational principle of democracy—is false when applied to nations. Men are created equal, but nations are not. There might be nothing wrong with democracy among the well intentioned, but when the membership of a global body includes dictatorships, terrorists, and Communists, there must be a means of distinguishing between those members who are willing to respect human rights and neighbors' borders and those who aren't.
- Membership: Any nation, pseudo-nation, or thugocracy, such as Iran under the mullahs, can be a member of the UN. Under Article 4, if the Security Council recommends admission and the General Assembly approves the recommendation, the nation becomes a member. Unless the Security Council recommends it, no nation can have its UN membership suspended or taken away.[9] In practical terms, that doesn't work. When a legitimate government is overthrown by a totalitarian one, the totalitarians take the UN seat. Because Britain and the United States refused to support it in the Security Council, populous and economically successful Taiwan, one of the few real democracies in the Pacific, and a traditional ally of the United States, was expelled from the UN and replaced by Communist China.
- Accountability: Although the secretary-general is the chief administrative officer of the UN, the Charter creates no system of checks and balances on UN operations. The opportunity for corruption—illustrated by the Oil-for-Food program—is enormous.

But structural defects aside, the UN's failure has been shown by experience.

Does the UN Work?

It's fair to ask: Just what does the UN do? It's far easier to say what it doesn't do. It hasn't created a world at peace and, to be fair, nothing can. General Douglas MacArthur, in his famous 1962 farewell at West Point, quoted Plato: "Only the dead have seen an end to war."[10] But the UN fails in most of its appointed tasks, even the ones in which it could find success.

Many UN adherents still claim that the organization works. And—to be perfectly Clintonesque—we need to agree on what "work" means. For the UN to work, we shouldn't expect it to be merely an instrument of American policy. Rather, it must be a serious forum for debate and decision. In fact, according to its Charter, it was supposed to be precisely what President Bush asked it to be in 2002: a means for coalitions of nations to form, and thus to oppose—diplomatically at first, and militarily if necessary—aggression against any member nation.[11] The endless debates and the dealings with Saddam Hussein's Iraq prove that the UN failed in that task. As an agent of global coalescence to oppose and defeat terrorism, the UN has rendered itself useless. It is broken in almost every material aspect.

In short:

- The General Assembly is broken because its principal purpose has been shoved aside in favor of political polemics designed to degrade the influence of the United States and its allies.
- The Security Council is broken because the alliances upon which it was founded no longer exist, and the interests of the powers that have a veto over Security Council resolutions have diverged to a point that consensus and action cannot be achieved.
- The secretary-general's office is broken because the incumbent is more interested in increasing the authority of the UN than he is in aiding its members in fighting terrorism or real

threats to peace. Supporting him in this, the bureaucracy of the Secretariat is dedicated to a Third World agenda that mirrors the dysfunctional General Assembly.

- Many of the most important UN agencies and programs have become so corrupt that they fail in their purpose, some even to the point that they aid terrorism.

The most obviously broken pillar of the United Nations is the General Assembly. As General Vernon Walters said when he became the U.S. ambassador to the UN on May 13, 1985, "The United Nations has become a place where many countries seek to achieve a lynching of the United States by resolution." Those resolutions come from the General Assembly.

The General Assembly

There was a memorable scene in the Japanese parliament in 2003. Considering a resolution to send troops to participate in rebuilding post-Saddam Iraq, the delegates debated, exchanged papers, and then climbed over their desks and punched each other out. That model of decorum would be an improvement for the General Assembly. Under the UN Charter, the General Assembly is supposed to be a forum for debate of any issues that may affect the peace and security of the world (and for debate over the UN budget).[12] It might be able to do that if its rules didn't allow every kakistocracy to join and vote. The UN changed for the worse in 1968, when the Third World nations figured out that through sheer numbers they could control the UN General Assembly and use their majority to shakedown the United States, Britain, Japan, and other developed nations.

They formed the "Group of 77," and in 1973, at a conference in Algiers, under the leadership of Mexican president Luis Echeverría Álvarez, they declared economic war on the developed nations. Echeverría Álvarez called for:

...a New International Economic Order that would break the monopolies of the transnational companies of the neo-imperialist powers.... The Third World must look on the United States and the old imperial powers as its real enemies; the former colonies must struggle against the menace of cultural imperialism as hard as they once struggled against old-style imperialism; the poor countries must support the cartel of OPEC as a demonstration of Third World power, no matter how much its price increases hurt poor countries; the Third World must rail against injustice in two pariahs—South Africa and Israel—and accept injustice anywhere else.[13]

That ideology was quickly and thoroughly implemented. In its infamous 1975 debate, the General Assembly debated a resolution that declared that Zionism is racism.

One of the most vocal proponents of the "Zionism is racism" resolution was Idi Amin Dada, the murderous dictator of Uganda. Speaking to the General Assembly—without a boo to be heard—Idi Amin called for Israel's expulsion from the UN and its extermination, and made it plain that he thought the United States was merely Israel's tool.[14] The U.S. ambassador to the UN, Daniel Patrick Moynihan, put this debate in perspective in a speech to the AFL-CIO:

Every day, on every side, we are assailed [at the UN].... There are those in this country whose pleasure, or profit, it is to believe that our assailants are motivated by what is wrong about us. They are wrong. We are assailed because of what is right about us. We are assailed because we are a democracy.... It is no accident that on Wednesday His Excellency Field Marshal Al Hadji Idi Amin Dada...called for "the extinction of Israel as a state." And it is no accident,

I fear, that this "racist murderer"...is head of the Organization of African Unity. For Israel is a democracy and it is
simply the fact that despotisms will seek whatever opportu-
nities come to hand to destroy that which threatens them
most, which is democracy.[15]

The "Zionism is racism" resolution was passed by the General
Assembly by a vote of 72 to 35, with thirty-two abstentions.[16] President Ronald Reagan, in a speech to the General Assembly in 1983, told
that body what its problem was: "The founders of the United Nations
expected that member nations would behave and vote as individuals
after they weighed the merits of an issue—rather like a great, global
town meeting. The emergence of blocs and the polarization of the
United Nations undermine all that this organization initially valued."
The Gipper's words were pearls before swine. The game of verbally
lynching the United States is still too much fun for the General Assembly members to stop.

The agenda for the General Assembly meetings in the fall of 2003
contained hundreds of resolutions concerning human rights, civil
rights, and the rights of women and children (as well as one condemning the United States's 1986 raid on Libya, which was in retaliation for
a Libyan bombing of a Berlin nightclub patronized by American soldiers, many of whom were killed). There were also dozens of declara-
tions about a right to food, and other seemingly unobjectionable
measures. When it came to a vote on these measures, among the "no"
votes was usually the United States, and occasionally Japan and the
UK. Why?

One reason is that terrorist states, following years of Soviet practice,
often propose General Assembly resolutions worded in lofty terms to
make political points. For example, the General Assembly passed—by
a vote of 125 to 53—a resolution against applying unilateral political
or economic pressure against a member state. Voting in favor were

China, Cuba, North Korea, Egypt, Iran, Libya, Sudan, Laos, Russia, Saudi Arabia, the United Arab Emirates, Vietnam, and Zimbabwe. Voting against were America, the UK, Australia, Spain, Poland, Israel, and South Korea, because these "coercive" measures isolate and weaken states that support terror and proliferate WMD.

Another reason is the UN's "agreed language" rule. Once language is "agreed to," it can be endlessly reiterated. So when the rights of Palestinian children are affirmed (in terms that require Israeli withdrawal from the West Bank), those rights are restated in virtually every new resolution. In the U.S. House of Representatives, there is a rule requiring that amendments to any bill be germane to the general purpose of the bill. In the General Assembly, there is no such requirement, so many otherwise unobjectionable resolutions are full of language condemning the United States or Israel. This is why there are so many "no" votes cast by the United States.

Typical UN Mischief: The Internet Power Grab

The General Assembly's many committees are always on the hunt for ways to create greater power in the Third World over the economies and freedoms of the developed countries. The most interesting power grab in the works seeks to impose UN control over the Internet.

The Internet—a beautifully free vehicle for freedom of speech—began in America. Not in Al Gore's head, but in the fertile minds of that most gallant gaggle of RSGs (Real Smart Guys) known as DARPA, the Defense Advanced Research Projects Agency. Over the last decade, the Internet has become a force in politics because of its ability to reach millions of people. (My Internet columns on *National Review Online* and *The American Spectator Online* regularly generate reader mail from as far away as Thailand and Australia.)

Because the Internet is controlled by the commercial market, a great many despotisms have either blocked their citizens' access to it entirely, or allow only limited access (Free countries do the opposite, which is why terrorists use Internet "cafés" all over Europe and America to communicate with each other). To fix the "problem" of Internet freedom, the UN General Assembly passed Resolution 56/183.

Resolution 56/183 provided, in seeming innocence, that a "World Summit on the Information Society" would be held to develop "a common vision and understanding of the information society and the adoption of a declaration and plan of action for implementation by Governments, international institutions and all sectors of civil society." But in the language of the UN, this means that the UN would try to take control of the Internet. The "summit" itself will be held in November 2005 in Tunisia. (So far, the costs of the preparatory talks and planning for that boondoggle already amount to $9 million.)[17]

At an earlier Geneva meeting—at which a "declaration of principles" was drafted—free press paragons Vietnam and China fought against proposals by America, Japan, Canada, and the European Union to include references to online freedom of the press and freedom of information.[18] But the free nations insisted, and thwarted the UN Internet takeover, at least for now.

The Geneva declaration of principles is instructive. It echoes language found in every UN declaration, including, of course, that the secretary-general will study the matter and refer it back to the committee. Getting along, and going along, means that the bureaucrats buy year after year of work by sending their report to the secretary-general, confident that he will send it back for more work. Occasionally, they actually do finish a product, which ends up in a treaty or a resolution that hands the United States, Japan, and Europe the bill.

Home Alone

Though, obviously, Third World delegations represent Third World ambitions, the interesting thing is that most UN delegations get to New York, set up in their plush offices, phone home—and nobody answers. Many of their governments simply forget their existence. For governments to ignore their representatives is the rule, not the exception, for members of the General Assembly. At least that's what the CIA and the KGB found out back in the days of the Gipper.

Ambassador Jose Sorzano was puzzled at the behavior of many UN delegations, so he asked the CIA to find out how many of the delegations actually received instructions from their governments on how to vote and—just for curiosity's sake—suggested to his Soviet counterpart that he do the same with the KGB. A few weeks later, they compared notes.

The spies came back with similar reports. It was a surprise, even for the most jaded UN observers. The CIA found that only thirty of the then 159 delegates were getting voting instructions from their governments. The Soviets confirmed the CIA's finding and added that, of the thirty, only two actually read the instructions (and one of those two underlined).

So the idea that the General Assembly is of vital importance to the Third World is a myth. Like the rest of us, it could get along perfectly well without the UN. The Security Council, however, is another matter entirely.

The Day the Security Council Died

The Security Council, the most powerful policy body of the UN, is composed of fifteen members. Five are permanent veto-holding members: America, the United Kingdom, China, the Russian Federation, and (sigh) France. The other ten are elected to two-year terms by the General Assembly. In early 2004, the elected ten were Chile, Germany, Pakistan, Romania, Spain, the Philippines, Algeria, Angola, Benin, and Brazil. It was in the Security Council that the French killed the UN.

President Bush had set Monday, March 10, 2003, as the deadline for UN action to authorize enforcement of its resolutions to disarm Saddam Hussein's Iraq. As that Monday dawned, French prime minister Jacques Chirac called for a later meeting of the Security Council to further debate the continued inspections of Iraq by UNMOVIC. At about 10 a.m., Colin Powell announced that the time for diplomacy had passed, and that we wouldn't even seek a UN vote on what would have been the eighteenth UN "disarm Saddam" resolution. On March 18, coalition forces slashed into Iraq.

The UN Security Council is hopelessly divided. On one side are the United States and its coalition partners, who are trying to stabilize Iraq and plant the seeds of democracy in the Middle East. On the other are the new Franco-German alliance, our Cold War enemies Russia and China, most of the Third World representatives, and an anti-American secretary-general.

It wasn't always like this—the UN Security Council, after all, was the vehicle of the "police action" to defend South Korea against Communist aggression—but the Security Council's decline into yet another anti-American forum was accelerated by two American presidents: James Earl Carter and William Jefferson Clinton.

Jimmy Carter thought the UN held America in contempt because America did wrong. So he appointed radical leftist Andrew Young as ambassador to the UN to apologize for America's many sins. Young, a civil rights lawyer and activist, criticized America for holding thousands of political prisoners, called our British allies and our Soviet foes "racists,"[19] and advocated the destruction of Western civilization, "to allow the rest of the world to really emerge as a free and brotherly society."[20] Jimmy Carter and Andrew Young made America seem weak, incompetent, and clownish in the UN.

The presidencies of Ronald Reagan and George H. W. Bush restored American prestige and even regained ground in the Security Council, which, in 1982, passed a resolution condemning Argentina's invasion of the Falkland Islands and calling for immediate withdrawal of Argentine forces.[21] Britain's forces did the rest.

Nine years later, when Saddam Hussein invaded Kuwait, the UN Security Council again responded quickly. It was clear to the United States—and to the eight other nations that co-sponsored our proposed resolution condemning Iraq's aggression—that Saddam had to be removed from Kuwait, and quickly. If he wasn't, he could have moved into the oil fields of Saudi Arabia and seized control of most of the world's oil. In an emergency meeting of the Security Council, the resolution was passed. It was the Security Council's fastest action ever to condemn aggression.[22]

But then came a new president—one who returned with much of Jimmy Carter's foreign policy team in tow. And he, like Carter, taught the Security Council and the General Assembly to believe things about American weakness and lack of resolve that simply weren't true.

CHAPTER EIGHT

CLINTON'S CLASSROOM

"Never apologize, mister. It's a sign of weakness."

—John Wayne as Captain Nathan Brittles,
She Wore a Yellow Ribbon

A SENIOR ISRAELI OFFICIAL WHO IS OFTEN ASKED TO SPEAK TO FLEDG-ling American diplomats headed to Arab countries told me one of the main lessons he tries to teach them is to never apologize, because the Arabs consider it a sign of weakness. It's a lesson that William Jefferson Clinton never learned.

President Clinton had little interest in foreign policy or national defense, and throughout his presidency apologized for one imagined American fault after another. Clinton never understood how the levers of American power could be pulled to move the world. Instead, because he was so uncomfortable in his role, he was content to let others take over for him. In the UN Security Council, and in Kofi Annan, he found men both willing and able to do so, and he chose to let them.

Clinton sent American troops to too many places—in the interest of "peacekeeping"—yet failed to respond with decisive action to direct attacks on Americans, our embassies, and even our naval vessels. His answer to terrorist attacks was to make meaningless cruise missile strikes, and combine them with bracing speeches unconnected to policy.

When policy was important, diplomacy was disconnected, especially in the Middle East, where the Clinton administration seemed to have no clue about the signals it sent. Clinton, for instance, taught Syria that it was possible to treat American threats with casual disregard. When Warren Christopher, then secretary of state, went to Damascus to see Hafez Assad, the Syrian dictator kept him waiting for hours before condescending to meet him. Neither Christopher nor Clinton understood the diplomatic damage done by accepting that insult.

Another example was the Clinton administration's treatment of Turgut Ozal, Turkey's prime minister for many years, who had been a faithful ally in maintaining Turkey's role as a cornerstone of NATO. Our most important Muslim ally, Turkey had stood by us when Iraq invaded Kuwait in 1990. Ozal acted quickly, cutting off the Iraqi oil that flowed through Turkish pipelines, while the Arab world refused to act, seeking an "Arab solution."[1] That hurt Ozal at home, but helped us significantly by cutting off one of Saddam Hussein's principal cash flows.

When Ozal died, neither Clinton nor Vice President Gore went to the funeral. In contrast, in an administration that really cared about foreign policy, George H. W. Bush's vice president, Dan Quayle, went to so many funerals that he was labeled "ambassador to the dead." The Clinton administration's insult to a crucial ally wasn't lost on Turkey—or on the rest of the region.

In defense and foreign policy, the Clinton administration gave the appearance that it had no idea what it was doing. Clinton made America's top defense priority not fighting terrorism, but forcing liberal social experiments on the military. Clinton's first secretary of defense, former congressman Les Aspin, was an absent-minded professor. As one source who knew him well told me, "Les would walk into every morning meeting and take all of the issues we had decided the day before and toss them up in the air again. Nobody ever knew what the hell was going on, and in truth not much did."

In the midst of this chaos, Clinton decided to let the UN use American troops again and again, in places where the United States had no national interest. He believed in global "interdependence," not American sovereignty. He taught the world that America could be a tool of the UN, and that the Security Council held the reins of American power. On September 24, 1996, Clinton told the UN General Assembly:

> In this time of challenge and change, the United Nations is more important than ever before, because our world is more interdependent than ever before. Most Americans know this. Unfortunately, some Americans, in their longing to be free of the world's problems and perhaps to focus more on our own problems, ignore what the United Nations has done, ignore the benefits of cooperation, ignore our own interdependence with all of you in charting a better future. They ignore all the United Nations is doing to lift the lives of millions by preserving the peace, vaccinating children, caring for refugees, sharing the blessings of progress around the world. They have made it difficult for the United States to meet its obligations to the United Nations.[2]

And he told the world how America was going to fight terrorism:

> The United States is pursuing a three-part strategy against terrorists—abroad, by working more closely than ever with like-minded nations; at home, by giving our law enforcement the toughest counter-terrorism tools available, and by doing all we can to make our airports and the airplanes that link us all together even safer.[3]

There was no hint that American action could take place without UN approval. As Michael Horowitz, senior fellow at the Hudson Institute, told me, "We had a president...who really believed that you had to shackle the United States because, after all, if you didn't it would fight another Vietnam War. The president of the United States was actively involved, as a matter of foreign policy strategy, in shackling and limiting the ability of the United States to act on its own as it perceived its own interest to be." As Horowitz said, Clinton would "see a problem, talk about it, sign a piece of paper, declare victory, and move on to the next problem, and leave the underlying issues festering."

From Haiti to Kosovo, American troops were put in the service of the UN, not in the service of the United States. Worst of all was Somalia.

Clinton's Somalia intervention made almost every conceivable mistake. It followed—almost immediately—the withdrawal of American troops sent there by George H. W. Bush under an earlier UN resolution.

In 1992, after his defeat by Clinton, Bush sent twenty-five thousand American soldiers and Marines to help distribute food to starving Somalis and to protect aid workers from murderous Somali warlords. Bush's ambassador, Robert Oakley, arranged a cease-fire between the principal warlords, Mohamed Farah Aideed and Ali Mahdi Mohamed.[4]

The Americans succeeded in calming the situation, their presence sufficient to drive the fighters out of the major city of Mogadishu. UN secretary-general Boutros Boutros-Ghali of Egypt wasn't satisfied, however, and insisted that the Americans disarm the warlords and their troops. Bush refused, and Boutros-Ghali agreed to his demand that a UN force replace the Americans.[5] Maybe it was because Bush knew that Boutros-Ghali had an old personal score to settle with Aideed; Boutros-Ghali had worked against Aideed while serving as an Egyptian diplomat in Siad Barre's Somalia.[6] Whatever the reason, Bush didn't allow the UN to take control of American troops or their orders. Most of the Americans were withdrawn by the time the UN forces—a conglomeration of troops from thirty-three countries—took their place. But the UN force, though much larger than the original American troop deployment, proved unable to handle the warlords, and chaos returned. President Clinton sent American troops back to Somalia for a brief and disastrous time.

The Defeat of Task Force Ranger

On the afternoon of October 3, 1993, a U.S. force took off by helicopter to capture Aideed. Major General Jim Garrison, the U.S. Army commander in Somalia, had asked for Abrams tanks and Bradley fighting vehicles to bolster the strength of his fighting forces, but was turned down by Les Aspin's Pentagon.[7] The raiding force—composed of Army Rangers and Delta Force operators—was some of the best we have. A rocket-propelled grenade brought down a Black Hawk helicopter, setting in motion a battle in the streets of Mogadishu that raged through that night and most of the next day. The fight dragged on because Garrison had no tanks or heavy vehicles that could penetrate blocked streets and incessant fire where the helicopter had gone down. Pakistani and Malaysian troops—who had tanks and armored vehicles—took hours to decide if they would brave the streets of Mogadishu to rescue the trapped Americans.

Eighteen Americans died in the battle and dozens were wounded. Television footage showed a howling mob dragging the body of a dead American soldier through the streets. Two days later, Clinton announced a reinforcement of the Somalia deployment, this time—he said—under American command.[8] He didn't even know the original force had been under Garrison's command. Shortly thereafter, Clinton announced that American troops would withdraw from Somalia by March 1994.

Clinton taught terrorists exactly the wrong lesson at Mogadishu, and his feckless policies repeated it, again and again.

What It Means to the Soldier

The day after the battle, my friend Dale McClellan, then a young Navy SEAL operator, landed in Mogadishu. He told me, "They were still washing the blood out of the Humvees when we got there." Images of American bodies being lugged through the streets were burned into his mind. Then he began learning some of the very hard realities of UN "peacekeeping" in the Clinton administration. Rules of engagement banned any offensive action; the accepted protocol was just to "shoot only if you're being shot at."

Spend my life if you have to, but don't waste it is part of the warrior's creed. In Somalia, however, lives were spent, but there was no intention of seeing the job through.

"I have a hard time explaining this to my mom," McClellan told me. "But it means everything to the soldiers, and their families. I talked a lot with the senior enlisted guys and some of our officers while I was in Somalia. They always asked, 'Why the hell are we here?' It seemed pointless. We knew the place was going to go back to what it was before we came.... Who wants to waste his life on something like that?" He puts it very well: "The least they can do is finish the job we went over there for. We never did that in UN peacekeeping missions. All those men died in Somalia, but what for?" As McClellan sees it, under President Bush, the bond between soldier and president has been restored. "I can go over there [to Iraq or Afghanistan] with a bunch of twenty-two-year-old kids or forty-year-old men, and we'd go with a smile, because there's a reason to be there. And we're not leaving until the job is done. That means everything to the men who fight, and the families of the men who die there."

By teaching the world that the United States would spend the lives of its soldiers pursuing the UN's interests—not its own—Clinton told our soldiers that their lives were of less value to him than the empty praise he received from Kofi Annan and the UN. He thus broke the bond that American warriors hold most sacred: a commander in chief's commitment to hold his soldiers' lives in trust.

Commander in Chief Kofi Annan

In 1995, Clinton—undeterred by the Somalia debacle—deployed American troops under UN command to Macedonia. One of those ordered to go was Specialist Michael New. New had no problem with going to Macedonia, but he had a big problem with the order that every soldier serving under UN command would wear the UN blue helmet, and that the U.S. flag patch on the right shoulder—by tradition, the most important on the uniform—would be removed and replaced by the UN flag, badge, and insignia. The U.S. flag was demoted to the left side. New refused, was court-martialed, and was sentenced to a bad conduct discharge. The court's choice was either to find New guilty or to find Clinton guilty of wrongly placing U.S. troops under UN command. The rest of the troops complied with the order, but the bitterness over that incident—and the distrust between the commander in chief and the troops—never faded.[9] Clinton's goal was achieved: America's subordination to the UN was clear.

Addressing the nation on November 27, 1995, Clinton talked about the UN intervention in Bosnia:

> When I took office, some were urging immediate intervention in the conflict. I decided that American ground troops should not fight a war in Bosnia because the United States could not force peace on Bosnia's warring ethnic groups.... But as months of war turned into years, it became clear that Europe alone could not end the conflict.

Clinton never explained what American interests were implicated in the Bosnian civil war. By the end of his presidency, Bill Clinton had reformed the world's image of America, and not for the better. There are three lessons he taught the global community:

- The UN, by determining where American forces should go, can be an effective means of constraining the United States in the exercise of its power.
- America will not respond decisively when it is attacked. Clinton took no decisive action in retaliation for the 1993 World Trade Center bombing, the 1996 Khobar Tower bombing in Saudi Arabia, the 1998 attacks on our embassies in Africa, or the 2000 attack on the USS *Cole*.

- Inflicting only a few casualties on the United States, as in
  Somalia, can defeat the United States.

These lessons, as the world has discovered since September 11, 2001, are false. One of the principal reasons we face the opposition we do today—in the UN, in Iraq, and in Europe—is that for eight long years, the world was taught to expect that America would subordinate its national interests to some other body, something America has—for almost 228 years—refused to do.

Today, we are paying a huge cost in blood and treasure to make the world unlearn what it was taught in the Clinton years.

CHAPTER NINE

UN REFORM: A FOOL'S ERRAND

*"There are many cases in which the United Nations has
failed....Justice cannot be a hit-or-miss system.
We cannot be content with an arrangement where
our system of international laws apply only to those
who are willing to keep them."*

—Winston Churchill

ON NOVEMBER 4, 2003, SECRETARY-GENERAL KOFI ANNAN ANNOUNCED a "high-level" panel to examine global threats and the UN itself, and to recommend whatever changes the panel believed were necessary to "ensure effective collective action, including but not limited to a review of the principal organs of the United Nations."[1] The panel is composed of representatives from France, Brazil, Norway, Ghana, Australia, the United Kingdom, Uruguay, Egypt, India, Japan, Russia, China, Pakistan, Tanzania, and the United States. The panel will labor for months and produce a mouse. Or, more likely, a rat. Annan has already told the panel what he wants: a Third World country, probably from among the Arab states, to become a permanent veto-holding member of the Security Council. This would make Security Council action against terrorists and the countries that support them impossible.

The bottom line is: Trying to fix the UN is a fool's errand, because in order to fix the UN, you need the cooperation of the states that are the problem. Some people, such as former ambassador Max Kampelman, argue that we should reform the UN by creating a new organization within it. In a January 6, 2004, op-ed in the *Wall Street Journal*, Kampelman wrote, "At a minimum, it is essential that the U.S. take the lead in establishing and strengthening a Caucus of Democratic States committed to advancing the UN's assigned role for world peace, human dignity and democracy."[2]

But this is pie in the sky. Let's say we formed a "democracy caucus" in the UN. It could be made up of the NATO member states, Israel, Japan, and a few other countries. And suppose we proposed an amendment to the UN Charter barring state sponsors of terror like Iran and Syria from chairing any UN organizations, including the Human Rights Commission and the Disarmament Commission. Suppose we also, as part of this amendment, barred the election of any state onto the Security Council (as a non-permanent member) without approval of the "democracy caucus." That would be real progress.

But such an amendment would have to be passed by a two-thirds vote of the General Assembly and ratified by a two-thirds vote of the Security Council, including unanimous support from the five permanent members.[3] Saddam Hussein has a better chance of returning to power than our resolution would have in passing the General Assembly and the Security Council. Of the 191 members of the UN, fifty, at most, have some claim to be democratic. And very few Third World, or even European, members of the UN want to give up what they think they have: a way to control the power of the United States.

British historian Corelli Barnett said in a letter to me that membership in the League of Nations in the 1930s bound Britain to take military action even where British interests were not at all threatened. In contrast, Barnett said:

> In 2003 the UN has the reverse function in regard to the
> US—to restrain it from taking action. From the perspective

of Europe, Russia, China and from public opinion even in countries whose governments support Bush's Washington (e.g., Britain and Spain), this potential ability to restrain the US is now the chief virtue of the UN.

Barnett's view is consistent with many who confuse the concepts of multilateralism with commitment to the UN and the need for, as Howard Dean put it, the UN's "permission" for U.S. action. America cannot and should not be isolationist, but that doesn't mean that we have to be multilateralist in the sense UN members want us to be.

The world's most vocal multilateralist is France's president, Jacques Chirac. His view is that the UN should hold sway over diplomatic and military action because without the UN, there is only the "anarchy of a society without rules."[4] His speech to the UN General Assembly in the aftermath of the Iraq campaign sets this out very clearly. Chirac speaks for the international elite that believes the UN has—as Barnett described—the proper role of constraining the United States:

> The United Nations has just weathered one of its most serious trials in its history: respect for the Charter, the use of force, were at the heart of the [Iraq] debate. The war, which was started without the authorization of the Security Council, has shaken the multilateral system.[5]

Chirac wants the world to believe that any action America takes is illegitimate without UN authorization. But Article 1, Section 8 of the United States Constitution gives Congress, not the United Nations, the power to declare war—a sovereign right that few Americans want to surrender.

In 1996, Senator Jesse Helms of North Carolina sounded an urgent warning about the UN:

> The international elites running the United Nations look at the idea of the nation-state with disdain; they consider it a

discredited notion of the past that has been superseded by the idea of the United Nations. In their view, the interests of the nation-states are parochial and should give way to the global interests. Nation-states, they believe, should recognize the primacy of these global interests and accede to the United Nations' sovereignty to pursue them.[6]

Unfortunately, much of Europe seems to have taken the side of these "international elites." So the West is divided. Underlying this division is a strong element of anti-Americanism in Europe.

British member of Parliament John Redwood has been called the Conservative Party's "lean, mean, thinking machine." He told me, "I do think the west is very disunited, largely because the principal engines of the EU are anti-American. In addition, old national divisions, and the traditional antipathy of the periphery for the centre in Europe create additional tensions. That is why the USA finds the EU so disappointing when it has something important to do, like the war on terrorism."

The West is split between a continental Western Europe that sees the world only in terms of trade and commerce—and that accepts terrorism as a part of life to be dealt with by law enforcement—and the United States, Britain, and the few other serious nations that see radical Islamic terrorism as a global threat as dangerous as Communism. The Europeans who are in denial about this have rendered the UN Security Council useless. In the words of Margaret Thatcher:

> For years, many governments played down the threats of Islamic revolution, turned a blind eye to international terrorism and accepted the development of weaponry of mass destruction. Indeed, some politicians were happy to go further, collaborating with the self-proclaimed enemies of the West for their own short-term gain—but enough about the French. So deep has the rot set in that the UN Security Council itself was paralyzed.[7]

And that is where it stands today. The UN Security Council is paralyzed by the disunity of the Western nations. The future of the Security Council was defined when France and Russia, owed billions of dollars from Iraq and eager to collect on sweetheart oil contracts they had negotiated with Saddam Hussein's regime, prevented any Security Council approval of action to enforce the resolutions they had previously condoned.

In short, the Security Council is broken beyond repair. America then has to face the question: What is our proper role in the UN from here forward?

Getting Out of the UN Game

A partial solution to the UN problem would be to get it to leave America. On September 20, 1983, America's ambassador to the United Nations, Charles Lichtenstein, suggested just that:

> If in the judicious determination of the members of the United Nations they feel they are not welcome and treated with the hostly consideration that is their due, the United States strongly encourages member states to seriously consider removing themselves and this organization from the soil of the United States. We will put no impediment in your way. The members of the U.S. mission to the United Nations will be down at the dockside waving you a fond farewell as you sail off into the sunset.

As nice a thought as UN departure might be, it won't happen. The UN building in New York City is owned by the UN and is regarded as international soil, so we can't just tell them we're taking it back and toss them out. They won't move—even temporarily—and we can't force them to.

But one thing we can do is end our UN membership. Indeed, that's what British historian Paul Johnson told me: "America should leave the UN and start from scratch with the democratic and law-abiding states." He added, "This might succeed because many nations would like an alternative to the viciousness and incapacity of the UN."

Johnson is right, but we can't simply walk out. America needs time to wean the free nations of the world away from the UN and into the new forum. To do this, we should withdraw from the UN gradually, in stages, and build on the growing UN disillusion in European, and even global, popular opinion (if not the opinion of European and Third World governments).

In its latest survey of world opinion, the Pew Foundation interviewed people in twenty-one nations, including ten in Europe. It found that:

> While there is a growing consensus that the UN has become less relevant, overall positive opinions of the world body have also decreased. The percentage of people who say the UN has a good influence on their country has declined in nations that took military action against Iraq—including Great Britain and the US—as well as those that bitterly opposed the war. Positive views of the UN dropped by 37 percentage points in Great Britain and 29 points in the US; the negative change was nearly as sharp in Germany (33 points) and France (28 points).[8]

To further this political climate change against the UN, we must end the pretense of UN control over the important issues facing the free world: weapons proliferation, terrorism, and the economies of the free nations.

First and foremost, no American president should ever again bring any serious issue before the UN Security Council. Consideration of any action we and our allies choose to take to defeat global terrorism is not a proper subject for UN debate. The Security Council and the secretary-general have to be made to realize that in our eyes—and in the eyes of the world—legitimacy comes from the rightness of the cause, not the blessing of the fifteen members of the Security Council.

Second, we could reduce the rank of our representative. Now, America's representative holds the rank of full ambassador, the equal of our representatives to real nations. Any representation of the United States in the UN should be by someone of lower rank. By reducing the rank of our representative, we reduce the UN's importance.

Third, we must shut off all U.S. funding for the UN—every penny—until the Iraq Oil-for-Food program is investigated to our satisfaction and the new Iraq Development Fund set up to prevent it from becoming just as corrupt as its predecessor. The entire UN—from Secretary-General Annan on down—should be investigated and any corruption revealed. Once that is done, anyone who has participated in the corruption—anyone—must be fired and charges against him or her brought in whatever court may have jurisdiction. The investigation and subsequent legal action cannot be taken under the aegis of any UN organization (including the International Court of Justice) because these organizations cannot be trusted to be impartial.

Fourth, we should take direct action against UN organizations such as UNRWA (which is a front for terror) that do active harm. A Security Council resolution (never mind that it won't pass) should be introduced, and a debate forced, on the matter of removing the heads of those agencies, starting with UNRWA's Peter Hansen, in order to expose what these agencies actually do and remove their credibility.

Fifth, we must insist that the next secretary-general—and all subsequent secretary-generals—be from successful, free, and capitalist nations; support democracy and human rights and oppose terror; and not come from the UN bureaucracy. Kofi Annan's term expires in 2006, and we are constrained by the UN rules on electing a successor. The UN Charter provides that the secretary-general is appointed by the General Assembly on the basis of a recommendation from the Security Council.[9] Tradition says that the secretary-generalship rotates around the world's regions and that no native of a permanent member of the Security Council can be secretary-general. Annan is from Africa. Before him, we had an Egyptian, a Peruvian, a Burmese, and three Europeans.

So the next secretary-general is expected to come from an Asian or Pacific nation.

Some conservatives want a secretary-general who will cast aside any vestiges of UN authority by his radicalism. It's not hard to imagine former Malaysian premier Mahathir bin Mohamad—Third World radical and anti-Semite—serving to sever even some of the world's elites' attachment to the UN. But this isn't the right course. We need to remember that the objective is to minimize the damage the UN can cause while we move ourselves and our allies into a new framework for international cooperation.

We should search, now, in countries like Japan, India, Singapore, and Turkey, to find candidates who share our values and who could help the UN regain a sense of reality.

New Alliances of the Free

If America is to lead the free nations out of the UN, we need first to define where we are going, and how we can get there. Our destination should be a new global organization of the free and democratic nations with which we share values and goals.

The new organization we establish must be outside of the UN, and be open to all nations that allow their people the basic freedoms of religion, press, assembly, and the others we cherish.

The new organization should not be created as a military alliance. Its goal would be to do what the UN was created to do, but is incapable of doing. We—and the other founders of this new global forum— can fix the problems of the UN from the start in a new charter. Such a charter should be based, as NATO's charter was, on the Atlantic Charter devised by Roosevelt and Churchill. The eight points of the Atlantic Charter (minus the sixth, which dealt specifically with the defeat of Nazi Germany) would be the starting principles of the new organization. In a form modified to deal with the threats posed not just by nations, but by non-state actors such as terrorists and their sponsors, the first principles of the new charter should be the members' agreement to the following:

- To seek no aggrandizement, territorial or otherwise
- To condemn territorial changes that do not accord with the freely expressed wishes of the peoples concerned
- To respect the right of all peoples to choose the form of government under which they will live; and to wish to see sovereign rights and self-government restored to those who have been forcibly deprived of such
- To endeavor, with due respect for their existing obligations, to further the enjoyment by all nations, great or small, of equal access to trade and to the raw materials of the world needed for their economic prosperity
- To work toward the fullest collaboration among all nations in the economic field, with the object of securing improved labor standards and economic advancements for all
- To enable all people to traverse the high seas, the sky, and outer space without hindrance
- To commit to the belief that all the nations and people of the world, for realistic as well as spiritual reasons, must come to the abandonment of the use of force. Since no future peace can be achieved or maintained if land, sea, or air armaments continue to be employed by nations and non-state actors which threaten aggression outside their frontiers, members must believe that pending the establishment of a wider and permanent system of general security, that the disarmament of such nations and non-state actors is essential, and the proliferation of weapons of denial and mass destruction must be interdicted and ended.[10] Members will likewise aid and encourage all other practicable measures that will lighten for peace-loving peoples the crushing burden of armaments.

The new charter would add an article aimed at the realities of changing governments, terrorism, and proliferation of missiles and other weapons and technology:

- To believe that the inequality of nations results not only from size, wealth, and military strength, but from the inequality of freedoms nations allow their peoples. Therefore, nations that allow the essential, God-given, fundamental human rights of freedom of religion, speech, security of the person and trial by jury, due process of law, the press, assembly, and the protection against cruel and unusual punishments, shall be entitled to membership. No nation shall, by virtue of the rights granted by its government at any one time, be entitled to retain membership if, in the judgment of the founding members, a successor government fails to ensure and protect these fundamental rights.

These beginnings of a charter establish a predicate for global cooperation without the indelible defects in the UN Charter. This charter would discriminate—openly and properly—against nations that fail to provide the basic human rights on which our nation was founded. It enables the member nations to consider seriously problems dealing only with peace and resistance to aggression in all forms, both of states and terrorists. It also provides the basis for establishing trade agreements among nations. This alone will be a powerful incentive to join, especially for nations such as Turkey that have been discriminated against by other non-UN alliances (e.g., the EU).

Gaining acceptance of this charter, and gathering members of the new organization, will take much time and effort. Every nation that joins cannot be required to first give up its membership in the UN. But gradually, as the organization gains adherents, and proves its usefulness in the ways the UN cannot, it will grow. And the UN will shrink in importance and in size.